Howdy, Duty!

An Insider's Guide to Navigating U.S. Customs

By Sandra Smith

Boskage Commerce Publications, Ltd.

Howdy, Duty!
An Insider's Guide to Navigating U.S. Customs

Copyright © 1998, 2002, 2005
by Boskage Commerce Publications
120 Cutler
Allegan, MI 49010

First Edition 1998
Third Edition 2005
ISBN 1-893495-36-1 / 978-1-893495-36-4

Printed in the United States of America
by BookMasters, Mansfield Ohio.

Dedication

To the Import Specialists of the U.S. Customs Service, who get precious little recognition or credit for the invaluable service they provide. The backbone of the Customs Service is its commercial operations division, and it is the Import Specialist who makes it work.

About the Author

Sandra Smith spent sixteen years with the U. S. Customs Service as an Import Specialist, Team Leader, Field National Import Specialist and Supervisor. In 1995 she left Customs and opened her own company, Import Consulting Services, to provide advice and training to importers, brokers and international trade associations, and taught classes in community colleges in both Dallas and Fort Worth. Her Broker Exam Preparation Class enabled many students to pass the Customs Broker Examination and obtain their licenses.

She has written numerous articles for international trade organization newsletters, as well as another book, *When You HAFTA do NAFTA: Practical Solutions to the North American Free Trade Agreement*, which can be purchased through Boskage Commerce Publications, Ltd.

After serving two large multi-national importer/ exporter/ producer companies as NAFTA Coordinator and Import-Export Compliance Manager, Ms. Smith is now consulting, training and writing independently.

Table of Contents

Chapter 4 - Classification Under the HTSUS
Howdy, Duty

Chapter 5 - Appraisement Under the Trade Agreements Act of 1979
Valuable Cargo

Chapter 6 - Special Provisions and Exemptions
You May Be Exceptional

Chapter 7 - Protests and Appeals
How To Get Your Money Back

Chapter 8 - Country of Origin Marking
Not Legally Marked - Marking Notice Issued

Chapter 9 - Other Agency Requirements
It's Not Just For Customs Anymore

Chapter 10 - Pre-Entry Rulings
See The Future

Chapter 11 - Fraud and Its Consequences
It's Not Nice to Fool Customs

Chapter 12 - Importing Textiles
The Fabric of Society

Chapter 13 - Other Special Programs
It's Bound to be Free from Somewhere

Chapter 14 - Intellectual Property Rights
Side-Step the Knock-Offs

Chapter 15 - Less-Common Laws and Provisions
Esoterica

Chapter 16 - NAFTA
Not As Free as They Anticipated

Chapter 17- Cargo Security
A Safe Supply Chain

Chapter 18- Think Before You Speak
There Is Too Such a Thing as a Dumb Question

Appendix

Index

Introduction

One day during my career as an Import Specialist for U.S. Customs, as I was deeply immersed in the controversy of whether to classify leggings as "tights" or "trousers," I received a phone call from a prospective importer. The woman asked me a few questions about importing tobacco products and then hit me with her major query, "How many cigarettes can I bring back under my personal exemption?" I told her the personal exemption was 200 cigarettes. She hesitated a moment and then asked, "How many is that?"

After a few seconds of absolute silence, during which she probably thought I had gone on a coffee break (I was trying to figure out how to explain the concept of 200), it occurred to me that perhaps she meant "how many packs" or "how many cartons." Once we established that, she received her information, and hung up.

This particular phone call has come to mind numerous times as evidence that people calling government offices frequently don't know how to ask a question. They want information, but can't seem to articulate what it is they're after. They have a vague idea of where they want to be but no idea how to get there. Some of them don't know enough about the subject at hand to know what questions to ask.

This book is not intended to be a complete synopsis of all laws and regulations for all merchandise. Rather, I hope to provide a handbook to serve as a general guide to the more universal of the Customs laws - classification and valuation of merchandise, country of origin marking, review and appeals procedures, etc. Importers need to be aware of the many rules, regulations, situations and exceptions pertaining to foreign-made goods. For merchandise-specific (and more detailed) information, importers should contact U.S. Customs, a Customs Broker, an attorney or a consultant, particularly since laws and regulations are constantly changing. Well, some of them change - the regulation requiring ship captains to declare to Customs the number of cannons on board their vessels did not change until 1993, with the passage of the Customs Modernization Act!

This book should also make it clear that importers must know all the details about the products they plan to import so they can answer questions asked by Customs officials.

In the government reorganization that followed the terrorist attack of September 11, 2001, the U.S. Customs Service was renamed Customs and Border Protection under the Department of Homeland Security. In this book, I still refer to it as "Customs." It remains the most complex agency in the federal government, enforcing over 600 laws for 60 different federal and state agencies. In addition to their anti-terrorist duties, Customs officers are concerned with everything from the flammability of children's pajamas to the lead content of china dishes. All imported merchandise is subject to a variety of laws and regulations, trade agreements, duties and fees. Hopefully this book will help importers of all sizes cope with the maze that is Customs clearance.

Icons

We've highlighted certain passages which represent key concepts with the icons shown below. In each case, the pertinent passage is indicated in italics.

 A point of law, generally giving the legal reference.

 Hints or ideas to remember.

 Time-sensitive information: deadlines or time frames.

 Definitions of terms or procedures.

 Important points to remember.

Chapter One

The Customs Modernization Act

Times, They Are A-Changing

What is the "Mod Act?"

*F*or over two hundred years U.S. Customs has been the guardian of America's trade laws. Two hundred years of practice has resulted in an agency that does a very good job with limited resources. They've also had that length of time to complicate matters, and they've done a darn good job of that, too.

As more and more state and federal agencies get involved in regulating products, the amount of documentation required from importers increases. Some Customs offices are knee-deep in paper and Federal Records Centers are overflowing with documents that must be retained for several years.

A few years ago, U.S. Customs realized that the old system of importing merchandise needed to be modernized. The Commissioner of Customs at that time, William Von Raab, whose battle cry was "Automate or Perish!" brought an agency with virtually no computers to a point where almost every employee had a PC on his or her desk. After the initial bugs were worked out in the new Automated Commercial System (ACS), it became obvious that Commissioner Von

Raab was on the right track. The main problem was that, after ten years of automating, electronic filing of entries was not technically legal. The Automated Commercial System was still designated as a test program.

Legislation was needed to repeal obsolete laws and allow for computer-age processing of entries. After several attempts to get the bill through Congress on its own, the Customs Modernization Act was finally tacked onto the back of another bill that looked as if it would pass – NAFTA. Officially known as "The North American Free Trade Agreement, Title VI – Customs Modernization" (and more informally as the "Mod Act"), this law significantly impacts both Customs and the importing public.

The main purpose of the Mod Act is to streamline and automate the U.S. Customs Service, improve compliance with trade laws and provide safeguards, uniformity and "due process" to importers. Some antiquated sections of previous laws were dropped or revised and, as a result, captains no longer need to report the number of cannons on board their ships before being cleared by Customs. The Mod Act officially introduces the controversial concepts of "informed compliance" and "reasonable care." The Customs Service is now obligated to communicate to the public what the laws are and the public is expected to exert reasonable care in complying with those laws. All importers, beginners and old hands alike, must be familiar with the Mod Act and how it impacts their businesses.

There are numerous Titles, Subtitles and Parts of the Mod Act, and each is important since your import operation will fall under several specific provisions. **The entire text of the Mod Act is published in Public Law 103-182, Dec. 8, 1993 (107 Stat.. 2057),** but for the purpose of this book only the more generally applicable sections will be discussed. The titles of each section are included at Appendix A-1.

Informed Compliance

*R*eferences in the Mod Act and accompanying documents to "informed compliance" are vague, and currently it isn't clear exactly how Customs is supposed to "inform" the importer so that he can "comply." They are required to issue regulations, administrative rulings, interpretations and other publications, both printed and electronic. It's up to the importer to find and utilize this information. The Mod Act assumes most importers are honest and in compliance with the laws. However, this compliance must derive from in-house expertise or from guidance provided by a qualified outside source. The importer must seek training for its employees and stay abreast of changes to laws, regulations and procedures.

Some sources of training are:

Colleges and universities offering classes in international trade.

Customs seminars and satellite-based training sessions.

Publications such as the Federal Register, Customs Bulletin & Decisions, etc.

International trade associations and organizations.

Customs Brokers, attorneys, CPAs and consultants.

Informed compliance and reasonable care are inextricably intertwined. Most of the responsibility for classifying and valuing imported goods now falls on the importer instead of Customs. It is no longer prudent to rely solely on your Customs Broker to "do things right." The wise importer has a good overall knowledge of Customs requirements and ensures that all rules are being observed.

Reasonable Care

*T*he term "reasonable care" is not officially defined in the Act. In fact, so many terms are not defined that this law is also called the "Lawyers' Relief Act of 1993" because of the years of litigation opportunities it will undoubtedly provide.

A few examples of actions which might establish reasonable care in certain situations are:

Knowing your merchandise and the terms of your transactions.

Being familiar with import laws, regulations, rulings and procedures.

Seeking advice from a Customs Broker, attorney, consultant or other expert.

Coordinating actions of intra-company divisions.

Obtaining laboratory analyses or other technical expert opinions.

Obtaining binding rulings from U.S. Customs.

Attending appropriate training and training company employees.

Instituting procedures to ensure accurate information is provided to Customs.

Establishing a cargo security system

Developing a system of internal controls/audits

Ensuring the adequacy of the recordkeeping program

Customs has published a "Reasonable Care Checklist" which asks detailed questions about import operations (see Appendix A-2). Answering these questions will give an importer a starting point in developing a compliance program, but it is only a start. Importing is complicated and requirements depend upon the product.

The courts have defined "reasonable care" as being what a prudent business person would do in a given situation. Customs seems to interpret it to mean that the importer makes no mistakes. Almost any infringement of Customs regulations is considered lack of reasonable care. Importers, even if they employ a Customs Broker to handle import transactions, are ultimately responsible for the information submitted to Customs, and are liable for any penalties assessed for violations. It is vital to be involved with and knowledgeable about your import processes and procedures, and make sure your company is in compliance with Customs Regulations.

Recordkeeping

*T*he Mod Act requires Customs to notify the public specifically what records are to be kept relating to an import transaction, that is, the entry itself. A list of these records, called the "(a)(1)(A) List" can be found in Appendix A-3 of this book, and in Part 163 of the Customs Regulations. Check it periodically, because it does change as new requirements are added via trade agreements. Not all of these records must be kept by every importer since some documents pertain to specific products. However, commonly used records such as invoices, packing lists and shipping documents will apply to everyone. A different section of law – 19 USC 1508 – requires the importer to maintain all records and correspondence pertaining to shipments, which are "normally kept in the ordinary course of business," in addition to the records described in the (a)(1)(A) List.

So far, the recordkeeping requirements of the Mod Act don't seem too onerous, do they? Your records may even be kept electronically. The general time limit for maintaining those records is five years from date of entry. Some records are subject to different time limits, so check with Customs or your Customs Broker before destroying any document.

Now that you have all your records organized so they are readily accessible, Customs requires you to produce them on request. In the past, if an importer did not provide requested records, Customs had to rely on judicial enforcement (court order) to obtain them. Under the Mod Act, Customs may issue administrative penalties for failure to maintain and/or produce the records named on the (a)(1)(A) List. **A "negligent failure" may get you a $10,000 penalty and if you are committing "willful failure" you are liable for a**

$100,000 penalty. These monetary penalties are assessed on each "release," i.e., each entry of merchandise. If Customs asks you for invoices for ten different shipments, and you "forgot" to keep them, you could be looking at a penalty of from $100,000 to $1,000,000. Recordkeeping is very important.

Recordkeeping Compliance Program

*I*f you choose to become a "Certified Recordkeeper" you may voluntarily participate in the Recordkeeping Compliance Program. A manual has been prepared by the Customs Regulatory Audit Division in Washington, DC, describing in detail the features and advantages of the program. Briefly, the importer formally agrees to do certain things, including, but not limited to:

> **Demonstrate** knowledge of Customs record keeping procedures.
>
> **Train** employees.
>
> **Have** a written procedures manual.
>
> **Conduct** periodic audits of internal procedures.
>
> **Report** errors and changes to Customs.

In turn, Customs agrees not to assess the maximum penalty the first time you make a mistake.

The Recordkeeping Compliance Program is very complex, and will be very time consuming to set up if your company does not already have similar procedures in place. Although many of the described procedures make good business sense and should be part of your company's standard operating procedure, setting up the complete recordkeeping compliance program would be impractical in very small companies, because of the manuals that must be written and the necessary periodic reports to Customs. If you keep all your records and give them to Customs when asked, you will probably not run afoul of the recordkeeping requirements, whether or not you are a Certified Recordkeeper. You can obtain a copy of the Recordkeeping Compliance Handbook by downloading it from the Customs website, or order it on paper from the address listed in the References & Resources section at the end of this chapter.

Miscellaneous

Other sections of the Mod Act affecting importers cover issues such as:

> **The requirement** that Customs provide copies of lab test results to importers.

> **The requirement** that importers receive copies of investigation referrals.

> **Stiffer penalties** for false drawback claims.

> **Establishment** of remote location filing of entries.

> **Implementation** of reconciliation entries.

> **Payment of interest** on both refunds and additional duties charged.

These are just a few of the areas in import laws changed by the Customs Modernization Act. Be a prudent importer and familiarize yourself with all its provisions.

What Do I Need To Do?

Be familiar with the sections of the Mod Act that pertain to your company and product.

Appoint someone in your company to be familiar with Customs regulatory and recordkeeping requirements, and ensure the company is in compliance.

Keep up with changes in laws, regulations and procedures.

References and Resources

NAFTA, Title VI - Customs Modernization (Public Law 103-182, Dec. 8, 1993, 107 Stat. 2057)

Importer Recordkeeping Compliance Handbook

Customs Internet Web site: http://www.customs.ustreas.gov

Publications are available from Boskage Commerce Publications, Ltd.
(1-888-880-4088)

Chapter Two

Types of Entries and Cargo Examinations

Your Shipment Has Arrived

Introduction

*I*n ancient times, when trade between nations was just getting started, there were individuals who extracted tribute or tolls from caravans crossing their territory. Later, certain pirates would demand a percentage of a ship's cargo for allowing it to make port. Through the years, these collections became an expected, accepted part of trade: the "custom." The town of Tarifa in Spain became a strategic base for pirates and the tribute paid to them evolved into "tariff." Governments were quick to see that this was a fairly easy way to increase revenues, so they slapped uniforms on the pirates, called them "customs officers" and made collecting tariffs legal, as long as the government got its share.

That is a somewhat abbreviated history, but it is essentially why Customs is called Customs. Many importers think the pirate connection is very appropriate.

In today's trading environment the tariffs, which are your "duty" to pay on goods coming into the U.S. are fairly low, with certain exceptions. The total duty collected is a very minor part of U.S. revenues, so the main purpose of having a "customs" requirement is to enforce various trade laws. In order to do that, importers must provide certain information to the government, and this takes the form of a Customs "entry."

The prudent importer will contact Customs before their shipment leaves its foreign port to ascertain requirements. This chapter will walk you through general clearance procedures.

The First Step

*T*he carrier notifies you that your shipment has arrived in the United States, and you must obtain Customs clearance before the goods can be released to you. What is the first thing you should do? It depends on the value of the goods, the type of merchandise, and what laws and regulations apply to it. When I first started work as a Customs Import Specialist, and asked a question about a law or procedure, my team leader's answer was always, "It depends." I thought he was being evasive just to annoy me, but I soon realized there are no absolutes in this business. The application of every law "depends" on something - the product, the circumstances, or even the time of year.

There are several types of entries - Formal, Informal, Consump-tion, Warehouse, TIB (Temporary Importation under Bond), Rewarehouse, Government, Foreign Trade Zone - and others. These various types of entries are situation-specific, and it is recommended that a licensed Customs Broker be engaged for everything except the Informal Entry. Use of a Customs Broker is not required by law, but the filing of entries has become so complex that most importers do not have the knowledge, staff or computer interface to file their own entries. In the coming years, electronic filing will become mandatory, and small importers will either have to invest in the necessary hardware and software to do it themselves, or hire a company to input their entry information into the ACS, the Automated Commercial System (to be replaced in the near future by ACE, the Automated Commercial Environment).

What are Customs Brokers, and What Can They Do for Me?

I'm glad you asked that question. Customs Brokers transact Customs business on behalf of the importer, for a fee. They provide a myriad of services to the importer, including international freight forwarding, Customs clearance, problem resolution and delivery of goods to the importer's premises. They are licensed by U.S. Customs, and are accountable under law for providing these services in a competent, professional and legal manner. They are familiar with all the ins and outs of Customs clearance, and can usually get your shipment released expeditiously and handle any problems that arise.

A Customs Broker can:

> **Prepare the import** "entry," on paper or electronically.
>
> **Be present** at examination of goods by Customs, if required.
>
> **Solve problems** such as: inventory of non-invoiced goods, affixing country of origin marking, mutilating or destroying goods (if necessary), obtaining other-agency releases, etc.
>
> **Pay duty** and fees, and complete the entry process.
>
> **Deliver cargo** to the importer, or arrange for its transport.
>
> **Execute bonds** as agent for surety companies.
>
> **Respond to Requests** for Information from Customs.
>
> **File Protests** and Administrative Review Requests with Customs in the event of a disagreement in classification, value, etc.

Your time is better spent marketing your product than trying to file entries yourself.

Informal Entries

*T*his is the easiest entry, and you, the importer, can do it yourself with probably only one trip to Customs and the freight area. You should call your Customs office to find out what the local procedures are, because seaports differ from airports and border crossings in clearance procedures, and office hours are different from one port to another. Regardless of these differences, the entry procedures will generally remain the same. When a carrier notifies you that your shipment has arrived, you take your paperwork (invoices, packing lists, shipping documents) to the Customs cargo office, and the Customs officer will decide whether or not to examine the goods. In the simplest scenario, no examination is done, and you pay any duty due, obtain a "release" stamp on the invoice and/or shipping document, and give that release to the carrier that has possession of your shipment. The carrier then gives you the goods. You sell the goods, make a million dollars, retire to a south sea island and never have to work again!

What qualifies for an Informal Entry? **Most goods can be entered this way if the value (the total price you paid or will pay for the merchandise) is $2,000 or less.** Periodically, this amount is increased. Check with Customs for the current limit. Some products, however, have different "informal" limits - some food and leather products can be cleared informally only if the value is $250 or less. If the goods were manufactured in the United States, and are coming back here for repair, they can be entered informally if they are worth $10,000 or less. Most "personal" shipments - goods that will not be sold or used in a business and are for the personal use of the importer - can be released on an informal entry regardless of value. However, commercial shipments of textiles cannot be cleared on an informal entry, regardless of value. Again, call the Customs office nearest you and ask what the requirements are for your particular items.

Formal Entries

*W*hen the value of your shipment exceeds the "informal" limit, it's best to get a Customs Broker involved. A formal Customs entry is no piece of cake, especially for a novice importer. Interestingly, it always seems to be the first-time importers who want to try to do this themselves. Most often they regret it, because (and I am speaking from 15 years' experience of auditing entries) they never do it right the first time. They end up making several trips to the freight area or cargo office at Customs, release of the shipment is delayed, and there are storage charges and monetary penalties for exceeding various time limits. Whenever an error is made on paperwork, it is "rejected" and returned to the filer. If the importer is self-filing the entry, it is mailed back to the importer, which adds several days to the process. Customs Brokers have mail boxes in the Customs office, and their messengers check these boxes several times a day. A Customs Broker can correct an error on the same day it is discovered, thus the shipment is not unnecessarily delayed.

A formal entry generally consists of CBP Form 3461, the commercial invoice from the foreign seller to the importer (Appendix B), a packing list, a bill of lading or air waybill, a surety bond and other documents that may be required for the particular product. This entry package is delivered by the Customs Broker or importer to Customs. In some cases only electronic data is given to Customs and no paperwork is necessary. Customs personnel will review the paperwork or electronic information, and determine whether to examine the goods. If Customs chooses not to perform an examination, a release is given to the filer either electronically or on paper. The carrier can then turn the cargo over to the importer. **The importer/Customs Broker then has ten working days to submit the Entry Summary and pay the duty, fees and taxes due.**

The Entry Summary consists of all the entry documents used above, plus a Customs Form 7501 and any documents that were not available when release of the cargo was obtained. The CBP-7501 will describe the goods, show the tariff classification number and duty rate, and other information that is transmitted by Customs to the Bureau of Census for compilation of trade statistics. Duty can be paid on a per-entry basis, or, if the filer submits numerous entries in a month, via statement. Electronic funds transfer is also an option for large filers such as Customs Brokers, who meet all the requirements of this program. With the development of more automated programs for processing Customs transactions, more options for filing entries and paying duty will be available. Your broker can keep you informed about these changes.

 A surety bond is required for almost all formal entries. This bond can be executed by the Customs Broker, or the importer may obtain one directly from any surety company that writes Customs entry bonds. The amount of the bond must be sufficient to cover any future duty the importer might owe, or certain other charges that may be levied against the shipment. In the event that the importer refuses or fails to pay these additional charges, or otherwise fails to comply with the bond conditions, Customs may proceed against the bond and collect the amount from the surety company. Check with Customs or your Customs Broker to determine the proper amount and type of bond needed for your shipment.

Examination Procedures

*W*hat happens when a shipment is examined by a Customs Inspector or Import Specialist? Why is a shipment selected for an intensive exam?

Some shipments are singled out for no other reason than they are coming from a source country for drugs. These are usually containerized shipments, and may contain goods destined for more than one importer. Drug trafficking is done on a large scale by hiding the contraband in the walls and floors of containers, unbeknownst to the innocent importer whose goods are shipped in that container. Sometimes an informant has alerted Customs to the presence of drugs in a shipment. Occasionally, a narcotics detector dog alerts on a particular container or stack of boxes on a dock. What follows in an enforcement exam, and there is nothing an importer can do to expedite matters, especially if drugs are found.

 Another type of mandated exam, and one over which even Customs has little control, is **the stratified compliance examination.** This is a statistically determined, computer selected exam based on the tariff classification number of the merchandise in the shipment. (Tariff classification is described in a later chapter.) The General Accounting Office requires Customs to conduct these statistically correct samplings to justify operational objectives.

At this point, you may wonder whether narcotic detector dogs and computers are running things at U.S. Customs. To make the humans feel needed, there are other types of examinations based on Customs officers' experience, analysis of importing trends, or just plain gut feeling. These officers sometimes review the paperwork you submit, looking for anomalies. Bananas claimed to be from Iceland would probably elicit an intensive exam because Iceland is not a banana-producing country. If information on the invoice is obliterated or altered, suspicions would probably be raised, thus causing an exam. Or perhaps your particular merchandise has never been imported through that port before, and the Import Specialist wants to take a look at it before it's released. Furthermore, your shipper may have had violations in the past with other importers, and Customs is checking everything coming into the U.S. from that shipper. There are as many reasons as there are laws.

How long does it take to get a shipment released? Again, it depends on what type of entry you file, what the merchandise is, whether or not it will be examined, and how many mistakes are made by the importer or Customs Broker in filing the paperwork. It can be as little as one day after arrival (if everything goes right) to several weeks (if everything goes wrong) to "never" if you have no luck at all. **Just be sure when you order merchandise from a** **foreign country that you allow plenty of time to clear Customs.** I received more than a few calls during my

Customs career from desperate importers who had a trade show the next day, and Customs still hadn't released their goods.

The Perfect Entry

*I*t's sort of like filing your income tax return and NOT being audited by the IRS.

> **The carrier** notifies importer of arrival; turns the paperwork over to Customs Broker.

> **The Customs Broker** files the entry.

> **Customs** decides not to examine, or the exam results are negative.

> **The freight** is released to the Customs Broker, who delivers it to the importer.

> **Ten days later**, the Customs Broker submits the Entry Summary and pays duty.

> **The Summary** is "by-passed" and "liquidated." No further action is taken.

The Less-Than-Perfect-But-OK Entry

> **Customs** decides to examine the goods, and finds a problem with Country of Origin marking.

> **A marking notice** is issued, and the Customs Broker arranges for marking.

> **Customs** accepts the marking, and releases the goods.

> **After the duty** is paid on the Entry Summary, an Import Specialist looks at the paperwork, discovering an error in classification.

The entry is liquidated and a bill is sent to the importer for additional duty.

The importer pays the duty and no further action is necessary.

The Worst Possible Entry

The merchandise is unmarked, undervalued and some of it is not invoiced.

The Customs Broker is unable to contact the importer, who is out of the country.

The freight sits on the dock, accruing storage charges, and the importer has to pay "late filing" penalties.

The importer returns, to find that his merchandise has been seized, and the customers who were waiting for goods have purchased elsewhere.

The importer has to sell his south sea island retreat to pay for the penalties, storage and marking fees, the items are out-of-date when they are finally released to him, and he goes out of business.

The remainder of this book will show you how to avoid the Worst Possible Entry.

What Do I Need To Do?

Hire a Customs Broker to file formal entries for you.

When you order merchandise from abroad, allow enough time for Customs clearance.

Find out requirements for your product ahead of time.

Don't try to smuggle anything into the United States. It probably won't be worth the consequences if you get caught.

References and Resources

Importing Into the United States - a manual summarizing and simplifying import regulations.

Title 19, Code of Federal Regulations
  -Part 113 (Bonds)
  -Part 141 (Entry of Merchandise)
  -Part 142 (Entry Process).

U.S. Customs Commercial Directives & Reference Manual - Entry/Immediate Delivery; Instructions for Preparation of the CBP Form-3461 and Instructions for Preparation of the CBP Form-7501.

Publications are available from Boskage Commerce Publications, Ltd. (1-888-880-4088)

Chapter Three

Invoice Requirements
Telling It Like It Is

Introduction

*E*veryone knows what invoices are. They come every month from the electric company and department stores and the banks that issue your credit cards. Invoices seen by Customs officers are very similar to your electric bill, but are sometimes much more entertaining. As an Import Specialist for U.S. Customs, I've seen invoices for track frogs, oil flingers, pig stackers, gulp hoses, flour socks and even one for "two pails of truss picks." Try, if you will, to conjure up a mental image of "one impregnating machine complete with dancer, chains and small parts."

The commercial invoice is the most important document in the entry package. It is supposed to describe what is in the shipment, how much you paid for it and where it originated. Inspectors use the invoice when an examination is performed, to determine whether the contents of the boxes match the paperwork. Import Specialists use the invoice to verify the value of the goods, as well as the tariff classification. Therefore, all invoices must contain certain information to be considered acceptable for Customs entry purposes.

Considerations For Your Invoice

*F*irst, the invoice must be in English, or have an English translation attached. In addition, the invoice must contain:

The U.S. port of entry.

The buyer's name and address (usually the importer).

The seller's name and address (sometimes Customs will ask for the manufacturer's name, if different from the seller).

The date of the sale.

The consignee, if different from the buyer.

Quantities and weights.

Purchase price, currency used (may be in foreign currency, but must be converted to U.S. dollars at time of filing the entry), terms of sale.

Amounts for freight, insurance, commissions, packing, rebates, drawbacks, bounties, assists, discounts, etc., as applicable (see the chapter about Value).

Component material breakdown, if required (i.e., what the product is made of).

Country of origin (country where the product was produced, grown or manufactured), and complete description of the product.

Most of the above items are self-explanatory, but "description" will, of course, depend on the product. **The Harmonized Tariff Schedule of the United States (HTSUS) is the book that describes all imported products.** If your goods are not described by name in the HTSUS, e.g., "bolts of steel," they may be described as "other articles of steel, not elsewhere specified or included." Look up your product with the help of your Customs Broker and determine what information must be included on your invoice.

It is necessary to include enough information for a Customs officer to determine the correct tariff classification of the product. Therefore, the item must be described in tariff terms. Sometimes industry jargon doesn't mean anything to the person reviewing the entry. The importer may know what a pig stacker is, but the Customs officer will probably show the invoice around the office, giving everyone a good laugh, and then someone will draw a disgusting cartoon of what they have envisioned. The importer must be contacted to get a better description. Release of the shipment might be delayed while someone contacts the American Society for the Prevention of Cruelty to Animals to see if they are interested in this thing. It's important to provide a generic description of the product if the industry description can be misinterpreted.

If you are importing textile wearing apparel, you will need to show, among other things, whether it is for men, boys, women or girls, the name of the garment (e.g. shirt, pants, jacket); the fiber content by weight (e.g. 60% cotton, 40% polyester); whether it is knit or woven, and sometimes whether it is yarn-dyed or printed. If you import "bearings", keep in mind there are ball bearings, roller bearings, cylindrical bearings, bearings that aren't bearings, but are called bearings in particular applications, and infinite variations of tapered, needle, radial, linear and spherical bearings.

It is the importer's responsibility to present a correct and complete invoice to Customs. If the shipper makes a mistake, it will be the importer who suffers with delayed release of the shipment, inquiries from Customs, or possible penalties. **Make it clear to your shipper that you will not accept invoices that do not meet the standards of U.S. Customs.** See Appendix B for a sample invoice.

If the importer cannot obtain a commercial invoice prior to filing an entry with Customs, a "pro forma" invoice is acceptable. This is a substitute invoice that contains all the information required, but is usually made up by the importer rather than the shipper. This does not, however, excuse the importer from obtaining a commercial invoice from the shipper. **If the cargo was released by Customs using a pro**

forma invoice, and later the importer is requested to provide the commercial invoice, there will be a penalty if it is not forthcoming within certain time limits, usually 120 days. Remember those recordkeeping responsibilities.

The Customs Regulations (CR 141.89) contains a list of items that require special invoice information, usually because of the complexity of tariff classification, special programs or the need for statistical information. These products are listed below. If you plan to import any of these, check section 141.89 of the Customs Regulations to determine what extra information is required:

Aluminum/alloys of aluminum
Bags, plastic
Bearings, ball or roller
Beads
Bed linen
Ceramics
Chemicals
Colors, dyes, stains
Copper
Fish or fish livers
Footwear
Fur Products
Glassware
Gloves
Grain
Iron/Steel products

Machinery and parts
Machine tools
Motion picture film
Paper/pulp
Plastic sheets
Printed matter
Rolling mills
Rubber products
Textiles of all kinds
Tires and tubes
Tobacco
Watches and clocks
Wearing apparel, headgear
Wood products

For example, if you import printed matter (books, magazines, etc.) don't invoice it as "printed matter." The invoice must state what kind of book it is (dictionary, catalog, encyclopedia, etc.), whether it is hardbound or paper bound, the number of pages, whether it is a periodical or newspaper, how it is printed, the thickness of the paper...well, you get the idea that special invoice requirements are very detailed descriptions of the product in the shipment.

It is also vital that the invoice covering your shipment reflect the quantities included in the shipping boxes. It is common practice for suppliers to include free samples, extra merchandise or gifts in the shipment of your merchandise. This is acceptable as long as the invoice shows these extra items, along with their values. Anything in the boxes that is not on the invoice is considered contraband by Customs, and may lead to problems. Usually, if there are only a few items of low value, Customs will allow the Customs Broker or importer to amend the invoice to include the extra goods, and enter and pay duty on them. If there is a large quantity of uninvoiced merchandise, however, it could be seen as a smuggling operation to evade duties. Make it clear to your foreign suppliers that all goods in a shipment must be included on the invoice, even if you are not being charged for them.

An omission from an invoice can make it difficult for an Import Specialist to determine the correct value of the shipment. **Be sure your invoice contains the terms of sale (ex-factory, FOB, CIF, etc.) and all charges against the merchandise (materials, labor, freight, etc.) so that dutiable and non-dutiable charges can be ascertained.** Value will be discussed in more detail in a later chapter.

One thing that causes Customs officers to scrutinize your shipment more closely is an invoice that contains altered or obliterated information. If a mistake is made on your invoice, the correction should be made either by drawing one line through the error and adding the correct information, or retyping the entire invoice. **Red flags go up and alarms sound when Customs finds correction fluid or wide black marker lines on invoices.** I recall a case in which an attorney, whom I shall refer to as "Ike N. Cheatem" (of the famous firm Boyd, Dewey, Cheatam and Howe), defended his importer client by saying, "My client meant to highlight that information, but accidentally grabbed the black marker instead of the yellow one!" After that in the local Customs office, black markers were known as "Ike Cheatem highlighters."

Another very important document that must accompany the invoice is the packing list. This should describe the contents of each package in the shipment, and it must match the invoice, or it will make the Customs inspector very upset when he or she examines the goods. The packing list should be detailed enough so that, when the Inspector opens the box, there will be no surprises. Inspectors hate surprises.

Prior preparation will eliminate delays in clearing Customs, and preclude a Request for Information later.

What Do I Need To Do?

Find out what information is required for your product.

Be sure the foreign supplier knows what information must be included on the invoice.

Provide an English translation, if necessary.

Describe the product as completely and generically as possible. Assume the Customs officer is not familiar with your product or your industry.

Be absolutely sure the invoice and packing list correctly reflect what is in the boxes of your shipment.

References and Resources

Title 19, Code of Federal Regulations - Part 141 (Entry of Merchandise)

Publications are available from Boskage Commerce Publications, Ltd. (1-888-880-4088)

Chapter Four

Classification Under the HTSUS

Howdy, Duty!

Introduction

*W*hat is 7 inches thick, weighs 13 pounds and has over 2,500 pages? This is no joke – it is today's Harmonized Tariff Schedule of the United States, the residence of duty rates for imported products. We'll call it the HTSUS for short, although there's really nothing short about it. There are sometimes several updates per year, and the book can be obtained on paper or electronic media (See the References and Resources at the end of this chapter for information on how to order the HTSUS).

I can't help but believe that many famous U.S. Customs employees – Nathaniel Hawthorne, Edgar Allan Poe, Herman Melville, Pat Garrett – are spinning in their graves over how complicated things are today.

But you, the importer, have done the smart thing and hired a Customs Broker to file your entry for you. Even so, you should have a general idea of how duties are figured so you can provide your Customs Broker with the information needed to complete the paperwork. Actually, you should determine the amount of duties, fees and taxes that will be assessed before your goods are shipped from the foreign country. Knowing all your costs in advance is vital – you must know that you can sell your product for enough to cover those costs, and realize a decent profit. South sea island retreats don't come cheap, you know.

When you talk to Customs (or your Customs Broker or a consultant) about the rate of duty assigned to a particular item, the activity taking place is "classification." The HTSUS has a companion volume called the Explanatory Notes, which is larger than the HTSUS, costs several hundred dollars, and functions as an interpretation of the HTSUS. It gives examples of products included in the HTSUS provisions and it can be very helpful in tracking down elusive classifications. These two publications can help you double-check your Customs Broker's classifications and discover options the Customs Broker may not have time to explore.

The Tariff Schedule is "Harmonized" in the sense that most of the major trading partners of the United States use the same basic arrangement of tariff items. Theoretically, an item imported into the United States should carry the same HTSUS number (to six digits) as the item being imported into England. However, the duty rates are different for each country.

The HTSUS consists of ninety-nine chapters. The first ninety-seven chapters are the international divisions that all other countries use, and contain the classifications for all foreign-made merchandise. Chapters 98 and 99 are unique to the United States; Chapter 98 contains various special provisions, and Chapter 99 is the home of temporary legislative tariff provisions. These two chapters will be discussed in more detail elsewhere in this book.

The Table of Contents of the HTSUS shows us that the chapters are arranged in groups, or "Sections", according to type of goods and degree of manufacture. For example, early sections and chapters cover live animals, plant products and animal by-products, progressing to prepared food items and chemicals. **As chapter numbers get higher, the products are further and further removed from their raw or basic state.** Untanned leather appears in Chapter 41, and leather shoes in Chapter 64. Trees appear in Chapter 6, lumber in Chapter 44 and wood furniture in Chapter 94.

This logical progression also appears within chapters. In Chapter 73, we see sheet piling first, then basic shapes such as ingots and billets, then pipes and tubes, and finally "articles of iron or steel."

The "meat" of the HTSUS (besides that provided for in Chapter 2!) begins with the General Rules of Interpretation (GRI). These are the rules and procedures to be followed in classifying goods. And you thought you could just look up your product in the index! The GRI are used by all countries using the HTSUS. The "U.S. Additional Rules of Interpretation" apply only to goods coming into the United States. Appearing after the GRI in the front of the HTSUS are the General Notes (GN). This section contains legal notes, definitions, lists of countries eligible for special programs and the specific rules of origin for NAFTA goods. In addition to all these notes and rules in the front of the Tariff Schedule, each Section and Chapter has its own Notes. This may seem like a lot of reading matter - and it is - but it is the legal basis for determining how much duty you will owe.

The reference number in the HTSUS assigned to a particular product is variously referred to as the "classification number," the "tariff item number" or the "HTSUS number." In the United States this number is ten digits: the first four digits are the "heading" numbers, the next four are "subheadings" and the final two digits are "statistical breakouts." The HTSUS is constructed as an outline, with subheadings indented under headings, and statistical breakouts indented under subheadings. **An item classified at any "indented" location must meet all the requirements and descriptions of everything above it, all the way back to the heading.** There are about 1,250 four-digit headings in the HTSUS, with thousands of subheadings and statistical breakouts.

The "Rates of Duty" section is divided into three columns, headed "General," "Special," and "2." The "General" column, also referred to as "Column 1," is for the United States' most industrially-developed trading partners, such as England, Japan, France, Taiwan, etc. The "Special" duty column shows the rates charged against products from "developing" countries, or those with whom the U.S. has special agreements, such as Canada and Mexico (NAFTA). These rates are lower than the "General" rates. The very high rates shown in Column 2 are charged against goods coming from the last remaining Communist countries (Cuba, Laos, and North Korea). The factor which determines the duty rate is the country of origin of the imported product - where it is grown, produced or manufactured. Check the latest edition of the HTSUS for the current list of countries eligible for each special program.

The General Rules of Interpretation

*I*n my career as a Customs Import Specialist I was asked more than a few times if I could find a "better" duty rate for an importer. "Better" of course meant "lower." Unfortunately, those pesky GRI set out the procedure for shopping for duty rates. The first four rules must be applied in order, which means you can only get to Rule 3(a) by eliminating Rules 1 and 2. The GRI are reproduced at Appendix C.

GRI 1

*T*his rule says that the titles of Sections and Chapters, and the index and table of contents have no legal significance and are not used to determine classification. They are for ease of reference only. The rule further says that classification is determined by "the terms of the headings" and the relevant Section and Chapter Notes. This means that, if you are importing live horses, and there is (at the four-digit level) a heading that says "live horses," that is where they are classified, if there is no Section or Chapter Note that says otherwise. You need not resort to any of the other GRI. Alternatively, if you are importing bracelets made of textile, and the Chapter note for jewelry in Chapter

71 says that textile items are not classified in that Chapter, then you must look further to find your duty rate.

Some Chapter Notes don't make much sense, so you just have to take them on faith, and do what they say. For example, a Note in Chapter 5 says that hair from a cow's tail shall be classified as "horsehair." You can't always use logic and common sense to classify merchandise!

GRI 2

*T*he further you go in the GRI, the more complicated they become. GRI 2(a) says that when an article is named in the HTSUS, that reference includes that article in a finished or unfinished state, or in an unassembled or disassembled state, as long as the incomplete or unassembled parts have the "essential character" of the complete article. A bicycle kit would be classified as a bicycle; a knock-down table is a table for tariff purposes. An automobile without doors would still be classified as a car.

GRI 2(b) covers mixtures or combinations. Any reference in a heading to a material or substance includes mixtures of that substance with other substances. In other words, it doesn't have to be 100% of the named material. A "leather handbag," even if it contains metal fittings and a textile lining, is still a "handbag of leather" in the HTSUS. Or "milk," even though it is mixed with vitamins and water, is still classified as "milk." Rule 2(b) further tells us that, if you have this situation and there is no specific heading for the mixture or combination, you must use Rule 3 to classify your product.

GRI 3

*I*f you've stayed with me this far you will love rule 3. It has three parts. **GRI 3(a)**, in its own little convoluted way, says that, when a good is seemingly described in two or more headings, the more specific description takes precedence. The heading for "shavers and hair clippers with self-contained electric motors" is more specific than the heading for "electro-mechanical domestic appliances with self-contained electric motors."

However, if you have a mixture and the two ingredients or components each have their own heading, neither one is deemed "more specific" and you go merrily on to GRI 3(b). For example, let's say your product is a box made of wood and metal, and there is no heading or Note that describes it (GRI 1 eliminated). It's not unfinished or unassembled (GRI 2a eliminated). GRI 2(b) tells you to go to Rule 3. Now you have found headings for "wood boxes" and "boxes of metal." What to do? According to Rule 3(a), since both materials are named in headings, neither is more specific. Let's see what GRI 3(b) tells us to do.

GRI 3(b) is the part of the General Rules of Interpretation that is loved only by attorneys, because it provides fall-back litigation potential in case the Mod Act is not sufficient for their needs. Remember back in Rule 2(a) where "essential character" was mentioned? Rule 3(b) involves the essential character of mixtures and sets. It says that, if you can't classify according to any of the preceding rules, a mixture or set "shall be classified as if they consisted of the material or component which gives them their essential character..." There was just one tiny little omission in the writing of the Harmonized Tariff Schedule. There is no definition of "essential character." This is why lawyers love this rule.

Let's say you are importing a glass vase, heavily decorated with silver filigree. The duty on glassware is eight percent, while the duty on silver goods is four percent. What would you say the essential character is? The silver, of course. But Customs would say, "Glass, of course." The importer's lawyer would say, "See you in court."

An essential character determination must take into consideration the nature and purpose of the article, the relationship and function of the components, the relative values and weights of the materials and a host of other factors. Let's hope there is a heading with your product's name on it, and you can stop at GRI 1.

GRI 3(c) anticipates the situation where no essential character can be determined. In this case the product will be classified in the HTSUS number occurring last (numerically) in the tariff schedule. For example, your box that is half wood and half metal, neither half being visually or functionally superior to the other, would probably be classified as a metal box in Chapter 73, rather than wood in Chapter 44.

GRI 4

You will probably never have to get this far in classifying your goods. I never encountered a single product that received its HTSUS number under GRI 4. This states that, if application of all the other rules fails to provide a classification, the goods will be classified in the heading for goods "to which they are most akin." The only example that I remember from Import Specialist school was a wine cooler. It's not wine, it's not fruit juice, and neither one imparts the essential character, according to Customs. (I don't know about you, but I don't buy wine coolers for the juice or water!) The decision was that the cooler was more "akin to ale and malt beverages than fruit juice, so it was classified as an "other alcoholic beverage."

Are you beginning to see why you should hire a Customs Broker to file your entries?

GRI 5

This rule is fairly simple and straightforward.

GRI 5(a) says that specially shaped or fitted containers (camera, gun, musical instrument cases) that are suitable for long term use, entered with the article, and normally sold with the article, are classified with the article. A camera case imported with a camera is classified with the camera. The value of the case is simply added to the value of the camera, and both take the rate of duty for the camera.

The only times these types of containers are classified separately are when (1) they are imported empty, or (2) the container's value is very high in relation to the item it contains, or (3) the container imparts the essential character. The twenty-dollar cases normally used with two-hundred dollar guitars will be classified with the accompanying guitars at the applicable rate for guitars. However, a shipment of five-hundred-dollar cases containing two-dollar guitars will take two different duty rates - one for the guitars and one for the cases.

GRI 5(b) governs "packing" and whether or not it is the usual packing for the product, or if it is reusable. This is a very subjective area and should be dealt with carefully. Just because packing is "reusable" doesn't mean it has to be separately entered and classified. The bottle you normally see at the liquor store containing your favorite brandy is "usual" packing and is classified with the brandy. However, if you're importing brandy in a crystal decanter, you're looking at separate duty rates, one for the brandy and one for the decanter.

"Usual packing" is classified with the imported item. Design of the packing plays a role. There is a ruling about a wooden cigar box that had Customs field officers shaking their heads. The box was very expensive, nicely finished, with no advertising or wording on it to indicate its use as a cigar box. It was obviously not going to be thrown away when the cigars were gone, so Import Specialists wanted it classified separately and marked with its own country of origin. The Headquarters ruling stated that, since the cigars themselves were very expensive, and the box was designed specifically for those cigars to protect them during shipping, the box was considered ordinary and usual packing for those cigars, and should be classified with the cigars.

GRI 6

This is the last of the international rules. The main idea here is that the first five rules apply at the subheading level, as well as the heading level. This rule also tries to make it clear that, when you are comparing descriptions to determine the more specific provision, you can only compare headings to headings, subheadings to subheadings, and statistical breakouts to statistical breakouts. You cannot compare a description in a subheading to one in a heading.

Nor can you compare subheadings in one heading to those in another heading. You must choose the correct heading first, without looking at subheadings yet. (I know, it's tempting, but be strong.) After you've selected the heading, then pick the appropriate subheading in that heading.

Additional U.S. Rule of Interpretation

There is only one U.S. Rule, but it has several parts. **Part (a)** says that "use" (other than actual use) is determined by the use in the United States, at or prior to the date of importation, of the same class or kind of goods, and such "use" will be the principal use. Principal use has been defined as "that use which exceeds each other individual use." This differs from the old law, which required the "use" to be more than fifty percent of all "uses." Now the "principal use" only has to be the highest percentage of uses, and may well be less than fifty percent. Got all that?

Say for example, you have a product (some sort of concrete) and the HTSUS number you want to use requires that the "principal use" be in the construction of buildings and other structures. The uses in the United States of your concrete are:

Construction of buildings	42%
Constructions of roads	30%
Maintenance of runways	20%
Other uses	8%

The "principal use" would be in "construction of buildings" because that's the highest percentage. By the way, if you get into a principal use situation, the burden of proof is on the importer. You will have to produce evidence of the different uses in the U.S.

Part (b) of the U.S. Rule is easier. This is the "actual use" provision. Actual use is satisfied if the use is intended at the time of importation, the goods are so used and proof of use is provided to Customs within three years. An example of this type of provision is the "agricultural use" heading in Chapter 98. Goods classified here are free of duty if you can prove (1) actual use, as described above and (2) that the definitions of "agricultural" apply.

Part (c) is the "parts" rule. Scattered throughout the HTSUS, particularly in the machinery area, are headings that include "parts of" the named product. This rule of interpretation says that "parts" cover products solely or principally used as parts of the named item unless (and this is a big unless) the part is specifically provided for itself. A water pump for a car is not an auto "part" because "pumps" have their own heading. A screw is not classified as "parts of machinery" because "screws" are provided for in a heading.

Commingling

*I*f your shipper sends you fifty different items, but invoices them as "miscellaneous samples" and charges you $1,500 for the lot, you do not have enough information to determine the correct duty rates. You have three options in this case - you can send the shipment back and no entry is filed; or you can provide your Customs Broker with a list of the items in the shipment with unit values; or you can commingle.

Commingling is a provision that allows clearance of a shipment to be expedited somewhat by charging the same duty rate on all the items, and eliminating that tedious list-making. Unfortunately, the rate of duty used by Customs is the highest rate applicable to any item in the shipment. (There are other options, but Customs likes this one the best, and the others are difficult for the importer to substantiate.) Always be sure your shipper provides an invoice and packing list with detailed descriptions and unit values of the items, to preclude expensive commingling.

 It is crucial to keep in mind that classification is not static. Rulings are occasionally revoked or modified, regulations change, importers sue Customs in the Court of International Trade and sometimes Customs even changes its own long-standing practices. Some of the changes can be tracked by reading the Federal Register or the Customs Bulletin and Decisions, or by searching the Customs website. Published decisions are also available by subscription from various sources. The easiest way to classify merchandise is to get a binding ruling from Customs, discussed in detail in a later chapter.

What Do I Need To Do?

The Mod Act places responsibility for classification on the importer. Learn how to use the Harmonized Tariff Schedule.

Give your Customs Broker complete information about the product(s) in shipment.

Keep up with changes in your industry that may impact your classifications and duty rates.

Keep up with changes Customs makes in rulings and regulations.

Secure unit prices for your goods so "commingling" is not required.

Get a Binding Classification Ruling in advance from Customs.

References and Resources

*Title 19, Code of Federal Regulations - Part 152
(Classification and Appraisement of Merchandise.)*

*Harmonized Tariff Schedule of the United States, USITC
Publication number 2937.*

U.S. Customs website - www.customs.ustreas.gov

Publications are available from Boskage Commerce Publications, Ltd.
(1-888-880-4088)

Chapter Five

Appraisement Under the Trade Agreements Act

Valuable Cargo

Introduction

*O*ne of the jobs of U.S. Customs is to collect the correct amount of duty. To do that, the importer must provide the correct value of the goods, since most duty rates are "ad valorem" – a percentage of the value. In addition, the information submitted to Customs in an entry or Entry Summary is used to compile trade statistics. These statistics are then used by various government agencies and industry groups for many different purposes. The United States Trade Representative analyzes import and export statistics and uses them to negotiate trade agreements with other countries. Labor unions might use the information to judge the impact of imported goods on specific segments of the U.S. workforce. Individual companies or trade associations can utilize the statistics to analyze trends, spot potential dumping situations and even tell what competitors are doing. It's very important that all the information, including the value of incoming shipments, is reported accurately.

The Trade Agreements Act of 1979 simplified the law by which the value of imported merchandise is determined. Even so, it can be an area filled with unexpected complications. In this chapter, we will cover only the basic provisions of the value law, pertaining to only the most common situations. **You should always consult with an expert to ensure you are declaring the total legal value of your merchandise to Customs.** It is better to declare it at the time of entry than to have Customs discover it later in an audit.

Transaction Value

The first basis of appraisement, and the one most commonly used, is "Transaction Value of the imported merchandise." This is the total price the importer has paid, or has agreed to pay, for the particular shipment. In its simplest form, Transaction Value exists when, for example, Importer Albert buys widgets from Seller Bob from a catalog or price list (or they negotiate a price), and pays in advance, upon delivery or at any time agreed upon by both parties. This is an "arm's length" transaction; nothing fancy happening here.

But wait. It can't be that simple. This is the government, after all. There is a little more to it, and there are a few twists and turns you can take and still be in Transaction Value. **This is the price paid or payable, directly or indirectly, when sold for export to the United States, with certain allowable additions and deductions.**

"Directly or indirectly" means the buyer/importer pays the seller or anyone else, by any means. You can't hide value from Customs by paying a third party, who then pays the seller. Well, you probably could, but it would be illegal.

Sometimes a seller settles a debt with the importer by invoicing only part of the value of the goods. For example, a previous shipment to Importer Albert was defective, so Seller Bob invoices the current shipment for half the real value, to compensate Albert for the defective merchandise. In this situation, the full value must be declared to Customs, because there is a settlement of a debt involved. There are infinite variations on the "directly or indirectly" theme so it's wise to consult with an expert about your particular situation.

The next condition of Transaction Value is "when sold for export to the U.S." This can work for or against the importer. If the importer is using a buying agent in Hong Kong to buy merchandise in China, then the price "paid or payable" is the amount the importer pays to the seller in China. The services of the Hong Kong buying agent are usually not part of the dutiable value. The goods were "sold for export to the U.S." from China, not from Hong Kong. Even if the merchandise is resold before it reaches the United States, the value will still usually be the original price.

To illustrate a sale in transit, let's say Importer Albert pays $10,000 to Seller Bob in China, and while the ship is still en route to the United States, Albert sells it to Chuck in Albuquerque for $15,000. Chuck decides to become the importer of record. Chuck is supposed to present both invoices to Customs, but he only pays duty on the $10,000 since that is the transaction that caused the goods to be exported to the U.S. The only problem is, will Albert want to give Chuck that invoice from the Chinese source? Does Albert want Chuck to know how much money he (Al) made on this deal? More importantly, will Albert want to reveal his supplier's name and address to Chuck? Rest assured, the next time Chuck needs these widgets, he will go directly to Bob in China and cut Albert out of the picture. In this example, poor Chuck will probably have to pay duty on $15,000, because he can't provide the other invoice, and Customs will gladly take the extra money.

There are five other elements of value that may be present in an "arm's length" transaction, which must be included in the value declared to Customs. These five items are affectionately known as "crapp" to auditors and Import Specialists:

> **Commissions** (selling).
>
> **Royalties** and license fees.
>
> **Assists.**

Packing.

Proceeds of sale accruing to the seller.

Commissions paid to an agent who works for the foreign seller or manufacturer are dutiable. These are "selling commissions." Commissions paid to an agent who works for the importer (buying commissions) are not dutiable, but must be declared to Customs. If you pay any commissions of any kind, contact a value expert for advice.

Royalties and license fees paid to the foreign seller are usually dutiable. These types of fees paid to a third party may not be dutiable. If you have Mickey Mouse tee shirts made by a manufacturer in Indonesia, and pay the Walt Disney Company in the United States a royalty to use Mickey's likeness, it would probably not be dutiable. But if that royalty is paid to the manufacturer, it would be.

Assists are very common in today's international trade activities. **An assist is something the importer sends to the seller or manufacturer in the foreign country, free or at a reduced cost, to use in making the goods that are being imported.** Importer Annie sends fabric to Seller Sam in India, who makes garments out of the fabric and sells them to Annie for a "cut-make-trim" price. Sam's invoice to Annie only includes the labor to cut the pieces out of the fabric, and make the garments. Annie must add the cost of the fabric (plus the freight to get it to India) to the invoice before it is presented to Customs. Yes, the value of the fabric is dutiable, even if the fabric was made or purchased in the United States. If Annie also provided the sewing machines to make the garments, the value of those machines must be declared to Customs as part of the dutiable value.

The regulatory definition of "assists" has been the subject of hundreds of rulings and court cases. According to 19 CFR 152.102 (the Customs Regulations), "assist" means any of the following if supplied directly or indirectly, and free of charge or at a reduced cost, by the buyer of imported merchandise for use in connection with the production or the sale for export to the United States of the merchandise:

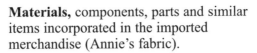

Materials, components, parts and similar items incorporated in the imported merchandise (Annie's fabric).

Tools, dies, molds and similar items used in the production of the imported merchandise (Annie's sewing machines).

Merchandise consumed in the production of the imported goods (oil for the sewing machines).

Engineering, development, artwork, design work and plans and sketches that are undertaken elsewhere than in the U.S. and are necessary for the production of the imported merchandise (clothing sketches and patterns Annie bought from a Paris designer and sent to the manufacturer at no cost).

The value of assists may be declared on one entry, or pro-rated over several. If Annie's sewing machines will be used for several shipments of garments, the value can be apportioned per garment or per dozen, so Annie doesn't have to pay the full amount of duty all at once.

If you are providing any of the above assist items, call for help immediately!

Packing is always dutiable, so be sure the invoice value includes the amounts charged by the seller for shipping containers and labor to pack the goods for transit. If your terms of sale are FOB, packing costs are included, but not separately identified.

Proceeds of resale which accrue to the seller are part of the dutiable value. If Importer Joe pays Seller Ignatz $5.00 each for widgets, and agrees to remit another $1.00 each after they are sold in the U.S., the dutiable value is $6.00 each.

Transaction Value rules also provide for several items which are not part of the dutiable value:

International freight and insurance.

Cost of construction, erection, assembly, maintaining or technical assistance for the goods after importation.

U.S. freight.

U.S. Customs duties and taxes.

If the above items are included in the invoice price, they may be deducted to arrive at the dutiable value. **Only the actual values may be used, though - not estimates.** To illustrate, a foreign seller invoices a shipment at $10,000 CIF with an estimated $1,500 for freight and insurance. But the freight bill shows an actual figure of $1,125, so that is the amount that may be deducted from the $10,000 to arrive at the entered value of $8,875.

Sometimes there are conditions which exist that might preclude using Transaction Value as your basis of appraisement. If there are limitations on the disposition or use of the goods in the U.S., or conditions for which a value cannot be determined, another method of valuation must be used. If the seller requires the importer to buy other goods to get the great price he's offering on widgets, that's a "tie-in sale" and it precludes use of Transaction Value.

Another situation that may or may not eliminate Transaction Value is the "related party transaction." Related parties are:

Officers or directors of one another's business.

Legally recognized partners in business.

Employer and employee.

One owns/controls 5% or more voting stock or shares in the other.

Parties owning/controlling or controlled by another party.

Members of the same family.

Relationships are slightly different if the transaction involves NAFTA. See Appendix D for a more detailed list of both NAFTA and non-NAFTA related parties.

If the foreign seller and importer fall under one of the above "related" combinations, Customs looks at the values a little closer than they would if the parties were not related. Being related doesn't necessarily exclude Transaction Value, but the importer must satisfy Customs that the relationship does not affect the price.

Transaction Value of Identical or Similar Merchandise

*I*f you cannot use Transaction Value for some reason, the next rule that must be considered is "transaction value of identical or similar merchandise." Say you've been doing business with Seller Bob for years, buying the same widgets at $5.00 each, and Customs has accepted this value. In order to reward you for your loyalty, Bob decides to give you today's shipment for free. (Sure, like this will ever happen!) Since there is no Transaction Value (no price paid or payable), you look at identical or similar merchandise.

"Identical" merchandise is identical in all respects, produced in the same country by the same producer and sold or exported at or about the same time. The price of last week's shipment of widgets, $5.00 each, can be used for today's free shipment, since they are identical widgets. If you have been buying the widgets from Bob, but foreign Seller Chuck sent you the free shipment to win your business, you still might be able to use Bob's price as "identical," because if the merchandise is identical, it may come from a different producer.

If you had no previous shipments of identical widgets, your value for the free shipment could be based on "similar" goods. To use a value of similar goods, the product must be "like" in characteristics and materials, and commercially interchangeable. **"Similar" goods can either be from the same producer, or another manufacturer.**

Deductive Value

*I*f you have no price paid or payable (and no Transaction Value), and there are no acceptable values of identical or similar goods, you must proceed to Deductive Value (or Computed Value, which may be requested at time of filing the Entry Summary). **Deductive Value is most commonly, but not exclusively, used when the importer is buying goods on consignment, and does not know at the time of importation how much will be paid to the seller.** In this case an estimated value is used for entry purposes, and the actual figures are submitted to Customs at a later date.

Appraisement under Deductive Value starts with the selling price in the United States, at the first level of sale after importation. Amounts for certain non-dutiable items are then deducted. Essentially, you are working backward to establish an FOB price.

Importer Frick agrees to sell foreign seller Frack's product in the United States for a commission of 15% of the U.S. selling price. Customs will start with the selling price and deduct the amount of the commission, international and U.S. freight and transportation insurance, Customs duties and taxes, and the value of any further processing done in the U.S. If the importer chooses, an amount for profit and general expenses can be deducted instead of the commission.

Computed Value

*I*f the importer wishes, use of Deductive Value and Computed Value may be reversed. **Computed Value is mainly used in related party transactions where "transfer pricing" is used.** Since this is a more complicated area than this book is intended to cover, suffice it to say that, if you are an importer using transfer pricing, you probably already know all about Computed Value. Briefly, this appraisement method arrives at a Customs value by adding the costs of materials, fabrication and processing, profit and general expenses of the producer, packing and any assists. Usually the result is either an ex-factory or an FOB equivalent.

A complicated twist in determining the value to declare to Customs is the use of "standard costs" or "standard pricing." In this scenario the values used on Customs entries are essentially fictitious because the actual costs are calculated at six-month intervals. This requires a Cost Submission to Customs twice a year to "correct" the values. It can result in a duty refund or an additional payment, depending upon whether the standard costs were too high or too low. Meet with Customs before you begin this type of operation to iron out the details.

Value if Other Values Cannot Be Determined, 402(f)

*S*ometimes importers think the "(f)" stands for "fantasy" value. This is the part of the appraisement law Customs uses if none of the other methods can produce an acceptable value. It cannot be arbitrary or fictitious. It must be based on one of the other methods, reasonably adjusted as necessary. Customs has great leeway in this section of the law, but they cannot simply pick numbers out of the air.

Currency Exchange Rates

*P*rimarily a clerical aspect of value, converting foreign currency to U.S. dollars at least deserves a mention. The Federal Reserve Bank of New York certifies exchange rates in use on given dates. If a daily rate fluctuates by five percent or more from the quarterly rate, that new rate must be used for that day. **Whatever rate is in effect on the date the goods are exported from the foreign country, is the rate used to convert to U.S. dollars.**

Too simple for you? Okay. If the date of export falls on a Saturday, Sunday or U.S. holiday, the rate of exchange for the previous business day is used. But wait - what if the previous business day has no certified rate? Use the quarterly rate.

Terms of Sale

*I*t's important to show the terms of sale on the invoice, because that's the starting point Customs uses to determine what should be added to or deducted from the price to arrive at the dutiable value. International terms of sale have changed in recent years, so be familiar with the current Incoterms. The most common are:

> **Ex-factory** - this price includes the cost of the merchandise plus packing only.
>
> **FAS** (free along side) - the price includes the cost of the goods, packing and the cost of transporting the goods to the conveyance in the foreign port.
>
> **FOB** (free on board) - the seller takes responsibility for getting the goods loaded onto the conveyance, and the price includes all charges to this point.
>
> **C&F** (cost and freight) - the price includes all the above charges, and international freight.
>
> **CIF** (cost, insurance and freight) - the seller has also kicked in the insurance.
>
> **CIFDPD** (cost, insurance and freight, duty paid, delivered) - the price includes, and amounts can be deducted for, international freight, insurance, U.S. duty at the correct rate, and any delivery charge to the importer's U.S. address.

As you can see, Customs value can be very simple (Transaction Value, price paid or payable) or very complicated (Computed Value, related-party transfer pricing). Check with your Customs Broker, attorney, consultant or Customs to verify your declared values.

What Do I Need To Do?

Become familiar with the Customs appraisement law – the Trade Agreements Act of 1979 – and how it applies to your business transactions.

Train employees in all areas of your company as to what elements of value need to be captured and reported to Customs.

State on the invoice the terms of sale and any required additions or allowed deductions.

Determine whether there is a "related party" element in your import transactions.

Give your Customs Broker complete and accurate value information to use in filing your entries with Customs.

References and Resources

Title 19, Code of Federal Regulations, Part 152 (Classification and Appraisement of Merchandise)

Trade Agreements Act of 1979 (19 USC 1401(a))

Publications are available from Boskage Commerce Publications, Ltd. (1-888-880-4088)

Chapter Six

Special Provisions and Exemptions

You May Be Exceptional

Introduction

*S*ince this is a book for commercial importers, it does not cover "personal" shipments. Anything that is imported for sale or use in a business is considered to be a commercial shipment for Customs' purposes. Commercial shipments are dutiable at their full value; there is no duty-free exemption as there is for purchases of goods for personal use, and brought back to the U.S. with you. Also, merchandise may be dutiable even though you have previously paid duty on it. A foreign-made product that is exported and re-imported is dutiable again, unless there is a specific exemption. There are several of these provisions that simplify entry requirements or lower the duty rate for particular products or situations.

 The following items need no "entry" and are not subject to the duty rates in the Harmonized Tariff Schedule. They are merely "declared" to Customs, either on your baggage declaration or a shipping document:

> **Corpses,** with their coffins and flowers.
>
> **Telecommunications** transmissions.
>
> **Business data** (records, diagrams, engineering/exploration data, etc.).
>
> **Articles returned** from space.

Items exported from the U.S., and returned as undeliverable within 45 days.

Certain damaged or unserviceable aircraft parts removed from U.S.-registered aircraft abroad.

Even though these items don't require entry, Customs does check these "exempt" items for contraband.

In recent years, dead bodies have been used to smuggle drugs into the United States by hiding the drugs inside the corpse. This is only slightly worse than the practice of having a person swallow a condom or balloon filled with heroin and waiting for it to work its way out the other end, a very common method of drug smuggling.

The "articles from space" exemption relieves astronauts from having to file a formal entry or proof of exportation for the Space Shuttle. This provision will probably be removed when interplanetary or intergalactic trade is initiated. A gentleman used to call me at Customs periodically to check on this. He said he was building a rocket ship and was going to salvage all the equipment that has been left on the moon by the Russian and American astronauts. He was having a little trouble finding investors.

Special Provisions in the HTSUS

*C*hapter 98 of the HTSUS contains provisions for reduced or free duty rates for specific products or situations. This is the first place your Customs Broker should look when classifying your goods, because Chapter 98 overrides the other 97 chapters. If there is a Chapter 98 provision for your product, it is classified there, even if a more specific heading elsewhere describes the good. Some of the most common provisions are outlined below. **This is not a complete list, so be sure you check the HTSUS before you import.**

American Goods Returned. If an item is made in the United States, is exported, and then returned without having been "advanced in value or improved in condition" while out of the country, it is not dutiable. You may have to provide proof that it was made in the United States by obtaining an affidavit from the manufacturer. (9801.00.10)

Foreign-Made Goods Exported and Returned. There are several headings that might apply to foreign goods that were imported, exported and are being reimported. These provisions cover such things as leases of equipment, goods that do not conform to sample or specifications, certain aircraft engines and goods exported for exhibitions or testing. (9801.00.20 through 9801.00.80)

Goods Returned After Repair/Processing. This subchapter provides a reduced duty for goods that are "advanced in value" or "improved in condition" abroad. The duty is usually on the value of only the foreign processing, repairs or assembly. This section requires proof of exportation, and in the case of assembly operations, very complex accounting records to substantiate the claim. Check with Customs ahead of time to find out what they will require. (9802)

U.S. Government Importations. If your company imports goods for government agencies, check out this subchapter. It provides duty-free status for merchandise going to the Department of State, military departments and defense contractors, the General Services Administration, the Nuclear Regulatory Commission, the Department of Energy, the Department of Agriculture, the Commodity Credit Corporation and the National Aeronautics and Space Administration. Some of these headings cover only specific products and others require evidence of eligibility, such as a government contract number. (9808)

Religious, Educational, Scientific and Other Institutions. Specific items are duty-free if the "institution" qualifies. Some examples are altars, gravestones and stained glass windows for churches; teaching materials for public or non-profit schools; life boats and life-saving apparatus; and certain scientific instruments if not manufactured in the United States. (9810)

Samples. This could be an important subchapter for your company, since it allows duty-free entry of samples of products that will be used for taking orders. The first two headings cover alcoholic beverage and tobacco samples. The third heading is for samples of any product that are either valued at less than $1.00 each, or are mutilated so they cannot be sold. (9811)

Temporary Importation Under Bond (T.I.B.). This heading covers articles that are imported temporarily for specific purposes. The goods must be exported within a year, but in some cases may be allowed to remain in the U.S. for longer periods if extensions are granted. T.I.B. provisions cover goods brought in for repair, for use as samples (of any value and not mutilated), for testing or experimentation, or for exhibitions. (9813)

There are many unusual provisions in Chapter 98, so be sure you or your Customs Broker explore the possibilities of duty free entry in this Chapter.

Chapter 99 of the HTSUS contains temporary legislation pertaining to specific products or countries. These provisions can either be advantageous or detrimental to the importer. Sometimes Chapter 99 mandates additional duty. For example, ethyl alcohol used as, or in, fuel has a regular duty rate in 2207.10.60 of 2.5%. The Chapter 99 rate is 14.27 cents per liter. You would pay both duty rates for the ethyl alcohol.

Occasionally, Chapter 99 allows a reduced or free rate of duty, such as for certain sweaters that are assembled in Guam. The normal duty could be as high as 33.8% of the value, but the Chapter 99 rate is "free" if all the conditions are met.

Chapter 99 is also the home of punitive provisions when the United States and its trading partners can't get along with each other. If the European Community charges high duty rates on California wines (or prohibits them altogether), the U.S. retaliates by charging 100% duty on European Community tomatoes. **There are hundreds of pages in** **Chapter 99, so if you are looking up duty rates for your products, don't forget to check the footnotes that reference Chapter 99 provisions.**

Regulatory Special Provisions and Free Trade Agreements

*I*n addition to the special tariff provisions in the HTSUS, the Customs Regulations contains numerous duty-free provisions and special exemptions. Many of them are so narrowly written, use of them is restricted to a tiny percentage of importers (barrels or boxes made from American shooks or staves, for example). Others have broad application, and we will discuss some of those sections here.

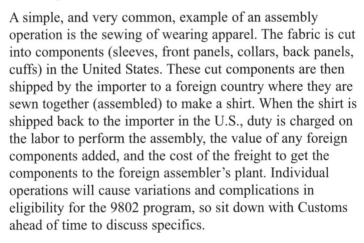

Articles Assembled Abroad With U.S. Components. We mentioned this briefly as a Chapter 98 provision, but the details are spelled out in Part 10.11 through 10.26 of the Regulations. **In the "assembly" or "9802.00.80" provision (previously known as the "807 Program"), duty is charged only on the cost of assembly operations and foreign parts.** The value of the U.S. made components is duty-free. Don't get your hopes up, though – that is gross oversimplification! There are complex documentary requirements, and certain manufacturing operations may disqualify the U.S. components from duty-free eligibility. See Chapter 15 of this book for more details.

A simple, and very common, example of an assembly operation is the sewing of wearing apparel. The fabric is cut into components (sleeves, front panels, collars, back panels, cuffs) in the United States. These cut components are then shipped by the importer to a foreign country where they are sewn together (assembled) to make a shirt. When the shirt is shipped back to the importer in the U.S., duty is charged on the labor to perform the assembly, the value of any foreign components added, and the cost of the freight to get the components to the foreign assembler's plant. Individual operations will cause variations and complications in eligibility for the 9802 program, so sit down with Customs ahead of time to discuss specifics.

Civil Aircraft. According to the regulatory definition, **a civil aircraft is any aircraft "...other than aircraft purchased for use by the Department of Defense or the U.S. Coast Guard."** This means foreign military aircraft

imported into the U.S. are considered to be civil aircraft. These aircraft are free of duty if the requisite certification is produced when Customs requests it. The certification, signed by the importer, states that:the aircraft (or parts) are imported for use as or with civil aircraft, and will be so used, and the articles have been approved for such use by the Federal Aviation Administration (or the airworthiness authority in the country of exportation.

There are a couple of other clauses about maintaining records and reporting changes to Customs, but it's a very brief (for the government) certification. Go ahead and import that Russian MIG fighter jet! Check with ATF about the armaments.

 Carnets. A carnet (pronounced car-nay) is a combination of entry and surety bond that is recognized in most countries. It allows the movement of shipments across national borders without filing formal paperwork. Most carnets allow merchandise to stay in a country for one year without the payment of duty, but the goods must be exported or be subject to a penalty.

Bonded Warehouses. Placing goods in a bonded warehouse is not really an exemption, but can be a way of postponing the payment of duty. In certain cases, merchandise must be entered into a warehouse and is not released to the importer, as in the case of a quota that has filled. Briefly, if goods are subject to an "absolute quota" only a certain number of that item may be imported during a given time period. If the quantitative limitation has been reached before the end of the quota period, any goods imported after that must be warehoused (or exported or destroyed). They must remain in the warehouse until the next quota period begins, or additional quota is allotted. Then they are "withdrawn from warehouse for consumption" and the duty is paid at that time.

 Another reason to warehouse a shipment is to take advantage of a duty rate that is due to be lowered in the near future. Duty rates are almost always reduced on January 1 of every year, so if your shipment arrives during the last two weeks of December (and you don't need it right away), it may be advantageous to warehouse it until after January 1 to take advantage of the lower duty rate. You must, of course, take into consideration the difference in the duty rates, and the additional cost involved in warehousing goods. Do the math, and you could save a substantial amount of money.

The United States has negotiated numerous trade agreements in the last few years, and it seems there are new ones every few months. The General Notes of the Harmonized Tariff Schedule contain descriptions of these agreements and specify the countries to which they apply. All of the agreements have certain requirements that must be met (for example, a percentage of originating value, or specified manufacturing operations), and some products are excluded. Refer to the specific General Note and the Customs Regulations for details.

When this book went to press, the agreements in effect were:

Products of Insular Possessions - applies to Guam, American Samoa, the U.S. Virgin Islands, Wake Island, Midway Island, Johnson Atoll and the Northern Mariana Islands.

West Bank and the Gaza Strip

Generalized System of Preferences (GSP) - applies to 119 developing countries, territories and associations of countries. See Chapter 13 of this book.

Automotive Products Trade Act (APTA) - vehicles and motor vehicle equipment from Canada

Caribbean Basin Economic Recovery Act (CBERA) and the Caribbean Basin Trade Partnership Act (CBPTA) - see Chapter 13

U.S.-Israel Free Trade Area - see Chapter 13

Products of the Freely Associated States - Marshall Islands, Federated States of Micronesia and the Republic of Palau. Refer to Chapter 13.

Andean Trade Preference Act (ATPA) - Bolivia, Ecuador, Colombia and Peru. Also see Chapter 13.

North American Free Trade Agreement (NAFTA) - see Chapter 16 of this book

African Growth and Opportunity Act (AGOA) - sub-Saharan countries

U.S.-Jordan Free Trade Area

U.S.-Singapore Free Trade Agreement

U.S.-Chile Free Trade Agreement

U.S.-Australia Free Trade Agreement

There are also duty-free provisions for certain pharmaceuticals, chemicals for dyes and certain vehicles manufactured in Foreign Trade Zones.

Your Broker can help you find any special provisions that might apply to your product, or you can take on the adventure yourself. Browsing through the HTSUS can be a very enlightening experience.

What Do I Need To Do?

Review Chapter 98 of the HTSUS. Alert your Customs Broker if any of the duty-free provisions apply to your shipments.

If you claim "free" entry because the goods were made in the United States, be prepared to prove it. You must be able to provide an affidavit from the manufacturer.

Check with your Customs Broker or Customs before exporting any shipment. There may be special documentary requirements if the goods will be returning to the United States.

Be aware of the special duty rates in Chapter 99 of the Harmonized Tariff Schedule.

References and Resources

Title 19, Code of Federal Regulations,
Part 10 (Articles Conditionally Free or Subject to a
Reduced Duty Rate)
Part 114 (Carnets)

Harmonized Tariff Schedule of the U.S. - General Notes and
Chpts. 98 and 99.

Publications are available from Boskage Commerce Publications, Ltd.
(1-888-880-4088)

Chapter Seven

Protests and Appeals

How To Get Your Money Back

Introduction

If you were the captain of a ship and a pirate tried to take twenty percent of your cargo, you might protest. Blunderbusses would be drawn and there might be swordplay or a few cannonballs lobbed back and forth until the matter was settled. Fortunately, protesting a Customs action today doesn't expose an importer to quite so much physical harm. You might get a few paper cuts from filling out the forms, but nothing life-threatening. Customs realizes that mistakes happen and they have a very comprehensive program of allowing the importer to obtain refunds of excess duties paid for various reasons.

This program is broadly referred to as "filing a protest," although a true protest is somewhat limited in scope. There are "protests" and "administrative reviews" and "appeals," depending on your situation. When I was a Supervisory Import Specialist in Customs, I saw every protest that was filed in the District. I once conducted an informal and unscientific survey of these protests over a period of about a year, and discovered some interesting trends.

About eighty percent of all of the protests and requests for administrative review were filed on entries that had "liquidated as entered," which means that the importer or the Customs Broker made the mistake and Customs didn't catch it, probably because the entry was not seen by an Import Specialist. Approximately fifty percent of all protests were "allowed," meaning that Customs reviewed the entry and agreed with the importer/Customs Broker, and refunded some money. Of the fifty percent that were "denied," about three-fourths were denied because the importer/ Customs Broker did not present any evidence to support their claim, and consequently no refund was made.

There are several types of reviews and protests, but they all have many things in common. They all have very definite time limits and are issue-specific. There is no required format for any of them, although CBP Form 19 may be used in certain cases. Multiple copies are required (five, if you want one returned to you with the assigned protest number affixed - handy if you ever want to track it down). Protests and other requests for review may be filed by the importer or consignee, the surety who wrote the bond for the entry, any "payer of exactions," a drawback claimant, and agents of these people – Customs Brokers or attorneys. In the case of protests concerning the North American Free Trade Agreement, exporters and producers in Mexico or Canada may also file protests.

19 USC 1501; CR 173.3

You might as well get used to it – the government speaks in legal citations. This citation in the U.S. Code is for the law that covers this particular type of review. The "CR" number is the section in the Customs Regulations where instructions may be found.

The first type of administrative review is initiated by Customs, under 19 USC 1501, covered in Part 173 of the Regulations. **This section of the law (usually referred to as a "voluntary reliquidation" or a "501 reliquidation") provides Customs ninety days after the date of liquidation to find and correct any mistakes.**

("Liquidation" means that Customs is finished with the entry and it is placed in storage.) Import Specialists may decide to look at entries for a particular commodity, or from a particular country, or for a particular importer (or for any other reasons); in other words, they "target" which entries they want to look at closely. The Section 501 window gives them the opportunity to pull those targeted entries from the liquidated files, and make any corrections necessary. Just because you get a Courtesy Notice of Liquidation telling you that your entry has liquidated at a certain amount, doesn't mean you're out of the woods. Customs isn't truly finished with your entry until ninety days after the date of liquidation.

19 USC 1520(a)(4); CR 173.4a

*T*he "520(a)" is a request to make a correction on an entry that has been submitted to Customs, but has not yet liquidated. The mistake must be a clerical error such as putting a decimal in the wrong place and paying $6,000.00 in duty when $600.00 was correct. It has to be a mistake that is made by a clerk "...upon whom devolves no duty to exercise judgment..." according to rulings by Customs. Errors in arithmetic are included in this section.

This type of review and correction is not very common for two reasons. First, most mistakes are NOT clerical in nature, and are not eligible under this provision. Second, most clerical mistakes are not found prior to liquidation of the entry. It is also sometimes difficult for Customs to find an unliquidated entry, so it's easier to wait until it liquidates and file some other kind of protest.

19 USC 1520(c)(1); CR 173.4

*T*he "520(c) claim" is technically a "request for administrative review" and not a "protest." This section covers only entries that are liquidated. The importer (or whoever is filing the claim) has up to one year from the date of liquidation to request review under 520(c).

The mistake must be a clerical error, mistake of fact, or other inadvertence, all of which have court-decided definitions. The definition of "clerical error" is the same as for the 520(a) claim: an unthinking mistake made by a clerk who has no responsibility to interpret any laws. Transposing figures, or copying something incorrectly from the invoice to the entry would be an example of "clerical error."

"Mistake of fact" means a mistake happens when a fact exists but is not known, or which is thought to exist, but in reality does not. When claiming "mistake of fact" the claimant must first establish which "fact" is at issue. For example, if the importer ordered giraffes, the invoice said giraffes, and it was entered as giraffes, but the shipment was actually zebras, that is a mistake of fact.

The last situation addressable under 520(c) is "other inadvertence." This is an oversight, involuntary accident, or a mistake made through inattention or carelessness. Keep in mind, though, that this section does not apply to the Customs Broker's or importer's mistaken or inadvertent lack of knowledge of the law or the Tariff Schedule, nor does it provide a remedy for negligent inaction.

 The snag in this section is that the clerical error, mistake of fact or other inadvertence claimed may not result in an error in the construction of the law. **In other words, if you or your Customs Broker has interpreted a law incorrectly, you can't get your money back under this section.** If the wrong tariff classification has been used for your goods, that is an "error in the construction of the law" so is not addressable under 520(c). That type of error falls under the next type of protest – a REAL protest.

19 USC 1514; CR 174

*T*his is the all-purpose protest. Almost any mistake can be corrected under this provision, as long as you request it within ninety days from the date of liquidation, or from the date of the decision being protested. A surety, or bonding company, protesting an entry has ninety days from the demand on the surety for payment. **All kinds of mistakes can be remedied here, including clerical errors, mistakes of fact and errors in the construction of the law, as long as the protest is filed with Customs within that 90-day time period.**

Issues may include value/appraisement; classification and rate of duty; other types of charges against the goods; denial of a drawback claim; exclusion of merchandise or demand for redelivery; liquidation or reliquidation; or a 520(c) denial.

The protest must contain a description of the merchandise, the nature of the objection, and enough evidence to support your claim. If it is practical to submit a sample of the item, do so, as long as it is not too bulky or difficult to handle. This type of protest can be submitted on a CBP Form 19, or in a letter, as long as all the information is present and in the same order as it appears on the CBP Form-19.

A word of caution about section 514 protests – always, always, ALWAYS request "Further Review." An Application for Further Review (AFR in government shorthand) ensures that, if the local Customs office denies your protest, it will be forwarded to Customs Headquarters for another look by an uninvolved party. Don't think that Customs people always back up other Customs people. There are frequently differences of opinion between the Headquarters personnel and the field officers, and about half the time, the field officers are overruled in favor of the importer.

To request Further Review, you must check the applicable blocks on the CBP Form-19 (or write out the information, if you are submitting your protest in letter form), and then make the statements that are required by the Regulations. You must state why you are requesting Further Review, and it must be for one of the following reasons:

> **The action** taken by Customs was inconsistent with a ruling or previous decision.

> **It concerns** a law or fact not yet ruled on.

You are submitting new facts on a matter previously ruled on.

Customs has refused to issue an Internal Advice on the matter.

You must state one of the above in the body of your protest, or on a separate sheet attached to the protest. Other factors which will merit a Further Review are:

Lack of uniformity of treatment (from one Port to another).

There is an established and uniform practice.

The matter involves interpretation of a ruling or Court decision.

The questions are not the subject of a ruling or Court decision.

The thing to remember is that you have to support your allegations. If you say Customs' action was contrary to or inconsistent with a ruling, state the ruling number in your protest, or attach a copy. If you say there is a lack of uniformity of treatment, attach copies of other entries filed in other ports showing the inconsistency. If ALL other ports are treating this issue the same, claim "uniform and established practice" and attach copies of entries.

If your protest is denied at the headquarters level, your only real option is to take it to the Court of International Trade in New York. **An importer has 180 days from the date of denial to file an action in the CIT** (there's one of those government acronyms, again!) and the attorney handling it must be specially certified to try cases there. If you are thinking of pursuing a matter this far, you will certainly need an attorney specializing in Customs matters.

If you think Customs has merely made a procedural error in denying your protest, you can request that they review it again, but you may not submit any new evidence to support your original claim. **The deadline for this type of review is ninety days from the date of the denial.** It is not intended to extend the protest period, or allow you to continue to disagree with Customs' position on the facts of the issue. This is available only to "...void a protest denied contrary to proper instructions...," the government equivalent of a clerical error.

Supplemental Information Letter

*L*ate in 1997, Customs implemented a new procedure that can be very beneficial to importers who wish to correct mistakes in entries. Before this new program was devised, entries liquidated as soon as the duty was collected and the time limits started running immediately. Then for a few years, entries were given a future liquidation date ninety days after input into the computer. For example, if the liquidation was done on May 1, the actual liquidation date would have been July 29 or thereabouts. The time limit clock started ticking on July 29.

Now the liquidation cycle is 314 days. An entry is collected and set up for liquidation, and the date is set for 314 days in the future. This is a nice length of time to audit entries for errors, both for Customs and for the importer.

The other provisions for protests and administrative reviews, however, have restrictions that make this 314-day time period unwieldy or unusable. Correction of an unliquidated entry under 520(a) is limited to a clerical error. All the other reviews are applicable only to liquidated entries. Customs realized this could create a hardship for an importer who discovered an error in classification, and would be required to wait almost a year to correct the mistake and get a refund of duty.

To provide a remedy for this situation, the Supplemental Information Letter (SIL) was implemented. This request for correction of an entry may be made any time in the 314-day liquidation limbo. Any mistake addressable under any of the other review sections may be corrected. It may involve either a refund to the importer, or payment of additional duties.

The procedures are fairly simple. The letter must be

submitted in triplicate to the Customs entry section in the port where the entry was filed and must contain the following information:

> **A list** of the entries involved.
>
> **The reason** for the requested change.
>
> **A revised CBP Form-7501** (Entry Summary) containing the "Tender/Refund" stamp affixed and the dollar amount shown.
>
> **Appropriate** supporting documentation or evidence.
>
> **A check** for any additional duty being paid.

Customs then assigns a control number to the letter, reviews it, and either rejects it for additional information, agrees with the importer, or disagrees. If Customs disagrees, the filer must wait for liquidation and pursue one of the other avenues for administrative review or protest. If they agree, the importer will usually get the requested refund without having to wait until the end of the 314-day cycle.

The Supplemental Information Letter procedures give importers extra time to discover and correct mistakes in their entries. But it also gives Customs that time to find errors. They can "unset" the liquidation during that time period and correct errors that may be detrimental to the importer. After a few years of using the SIL, Customs has realized that entry-by-entry corrections increase the workload for both Customs and the importer. In 2001 a procedure was devised for submitting a quarterly list of corrections. This is called a Post Entry Amendment (PEA).

Post Entry Amendment

*T*he PEA started out being a good idea. It enables an importer to account for small corrections on a quarterly basis instead of submitting a SIL for every entry. At least that's what you think when you start reading the PEA instructions. As you get further into it though, you discover that if you are due refunds on the entries included in this quarterly report, you must still file protests to get your money back. Also, Customs requires you to report small statistical errors that not even the Bureau of Census is interested in. So what is the point of the PEA?

It's only my opinion, but I think it's Customs' way of getting you to give them a list of your mistakes so they don't have to go to the trouble of finding them. Customs will use the list at some future date to establish lack of reasonable care. It does not afford you the same protection as a prior disclosure. **I can see absolutely no advantage to the importer in using the PEA,** so as long as it's a voluntary program, I'd avoid it.

In the last year or two, there has been a significant shift in Customs' attitude. Previously, the message was, "We know the laws are complicated. We think most importers are honest. We will try to work with you to ensure voluntary compliance." Today, the message is, "If we find your mistakes, we'll penalize you. If you tell us about your mistakes, we'll penalize you. If you are not error-free, you are guilty of failure to exercise reasonable care."

The PEA should actually be called LENTIL/BEAN: Little Errors Now Turning Into Large/Be Expecting a Noogie.

Why Are My Protests Denied?

*B*y far the most common reason why Customs denies a protest is lack of evidence to support the claim. Some protest filers seem to think the logic of their arguments is so crystal clear that Customs will have to see things their way. In some cases, the correctness of the importer's position is "manifest from the record." Customs looks at the entry, and sure enough, those giraffes were erroneously entered as zebras, and they will allow the protest and refund the money. Most of the time, however, the waters are murkier than that. In one protest I remember, the importer insisted that he had received flashlights instead of children's bedroom slippers, but submitted no evidence to contradict the shipping documents and invoices, which all said "children's bedroom slippers." Another example concerned merchandise which had been entered as being made in China, but the protest claimed Macau was the country of origin, and requested a full refund of duties under the Generalized System of Preferences. Again, no evidence was submitted that the product was actually made in Macau, or that it met the eligibility requirements of the special program.

Another common reason for denied protests is that the evidence does not match the claim. You'd be surprised how often this happens. The protester says those giraffes were really zebras, and here's the invoice to prove it - and the invoice is for gorillas.

 Frequently, the protest or other request for administrative review is untimely. **Adhere strictly to those time limits - extensions are rarely granted, and only for VERY unusual circumstances.**

Then there are the "frivolous" matters, which are extremely annoying to Customs, and are a big waste of the taxpayers' dollar. These protests cover goods which are not even in the entry cited in the protest; or the entry actually liquidated correctly, at the rate requested by the importer; or a protest was filed instead of a drawback claim; or there is a GSP claim for a non-GSP-eligible country; or any of several silly things. It is very time-consuming to process a protest within Customs, and numerous people are involved. I estimate that it costs at least $150.00 to handle a simple, one-issue protest that is forwarded to Customs Headquarters for Further Review. The more complex the protest, the more hours of highly-paid time must be spent reviewing it.

Take heart though – it's easier to get money back from Customs than from the IRS!

What Do I Need To Do?

If a mistake is discovered, notify your Customs Broker immediately.

Determine the correct type of request to file (administrative review, protest, supplemental information letter, etc.).

Be specific as to what you think the error is, and what correction should be made.

Attach evidence to support your claim.

Always request Further Review of a protest.

References and Resources

Title 19, Code of Federal Regulations
Part 173 (Administrative Review in General)
Part 174 (Protests)
Part 176 (Proceedings in the Court of International Trade).

Publications are available from Boskage Commerce Publications, Ltd. (1-888-880-4088)

Chapter Eight

Country of Origin Marking

Not Legally Marked - Marking Notice Issued

Introduction

*T*he country of Goodistan makes very high-quality widgets. The widgets made in Junkalia, on the other hand, are the worst in the world. They break, causing airplanes to fall out of the sky. No one wants to buy widgets made in Junkalia. But they look exactly like the good ones from Goodistan. How do you tell the difference? Well, there is that die-stamped marking on them that says "Made in Goodistan."

Country-of-origin marking is required by 19 USC 1304 and Part 134 of the Customs Regulations. The purpose of the marking requirement is to provide the U.S. consumer with information which can be used in the decision whether or not to buy a particular product. At one time, if something was made in Japan, people were reluctant to purchase it, either because of adverse reaction due to World War II, or because the products were considered shoddy and inferior. Today, Japan manufactures some of the highest quality products in the world, and the average household contains many such items. If your VCR isn't made in Japan, chances are your bicycle, computer or automobile is. Or your porcelain dinnerware. Or perhaps your patio furniture.

The Court has ruled that the U.S. consumer has a right to know where the item is manufactured, before the purchase is completed. The only way they will know this is if the product is marked with its "country of origin."

Inadequate or non-existent country-of-origin marking on imported products is the most common problem faced by importers. At the very least, lack of proper marking can delay release of your shipment; at worst, the merchandise may be seized and a penalty issued.

General Marking Requirements

The law says that imported articles of foreign origin must be marked with their country of origin (i.e. the country where they are made or grown) in a manner that is as legible, conspicuous and permanent as the nature of the article will allow. This is a very broad rule and there have been numerous court cases and Customs rulings to interpret these three requirements.

 "Legible" has been ruled to mean that the marking can be read in normal light without undue strain. This has been construed to mean you don't need a magnifying glass to see it. And, by the way, the names of the countries must be the English version, and generally abbreviations are not acceptable. There are exceptions, so check with Customs to be sure. For example, "Germany" is acceptable but "Deutschland" is not. "England" is okay, but "U.K." is not.

 "Conspicuous" means that the consumer can find the marking easily in a cursory examination of the product. A country of origin tag affixed inside the pocket of a pair of trousers is not "conspicuous" for Customs purposes. You should not have to hold a product at a certain angle to catch the last ray of sunshine to reflect off the country of marking. Cast-in-the-mold marking is particularly troublesome because it is often not in a contrasting color, and is hard to see. It is usually fairly obvious to Customs officers when marking is deliberately applied so as to be inconspicuous. Don't assume that just because it's there, the marking will pass Customs' scrutiny and meet the "conspicuous" test.

What constitutes "permanent" is a matter of interpretation, even more so than "legible" and "conspicuous." The marking must remain attached to the article until it is deliberately removed by the ultimate consumer. Except for a few specific items, there are no prescribed methods to ensure permanence. The nature of the article will dictate the method. Stickers, hang tags, and printing are all acceptable as long as the marking stays on the item through all the wholesale and retail levels of sale, until the "ultimate consumer" deliberately removes the marking.

Some items require special marking, or methods of marking. These special requirements cause the worst problems for importers because they are difficult and/or expensive to accomplish after the goods arrive in the U.S. Always call Customs to find out if your product is subject to any special marking requirements. Some of the more common special markings are discussed below.

Watches and Clocks

*T*his is probably the most troublesome of all special marking required. Watches and clocks are subject to two different marking laws, i.e., 19 USC 1304 and 19 USC 1202.

Briefly, watch movements (the guts of the watch) must be marked with the country where the parts are assembled, the name of the manufacturer or importer, and in words, the number of anti-friction jewels in the movement. The watch case (the part that holds the movement) must show the country of its manufacture, and the name of the manufacturer or importer. The movement and case markings must be etched, engraved, die-sunk, stamped or cast in-the-mold.

After the above special marking requirements are met, the 19 US 1304 law kicks in. The outside of the watch must show the country where the movement was made. The country of origin of the entire watch is considered to be the country where the movement was assembled. It makes no difference where the movement was put into the case, or where the band was attached. The band and battery must each show their own countries of origin. The only exception for bands is a situation in which the band is attached to the watch in the same country where the movement was assembled.

If you're going to import clocks, the movement has to be marked with the same information as watch movements, in the same prescribed manner. The outermost case of the clock has to show its country of origin on "the most visible part of the outside of the back" of the case. This could create a problem on highly decorative clocks that are designed to be seen from all sides. Before importing watches or clocks you should take a sample to a Customs office and verify that the markings are adequate. **Before you**

even order watches or clocks from a foreign source, send a copy of the marking requirements, which Customs can provide you, to your supplier, and make it clear that the product must be marked in the foreign country.

Textile Products

*M*any textile products, including wearing apparel, must be marked with their fiber content, country of origin and the importer's or distributor's "RN" number or name. The rules vary as to location and method of attachment, and the arrangement of information on the label. There are also many exceptions. For example, clothing labels must show the above information, and no other information (such as style number or size) may "interfere" with the required information. There is also other labeling (such as care instructions) that is not required at the time of importation, but must be affixed prior to sale in the U.S..

A mandatory reference for textile importers is the Textile Fiber Products Identification Act and its accompanying booklet of questions and answers. You will also need the Wool Products Labeling Act, and for good measure, the Fur Products Labeling Act. If you import textile clothing trimmed with fur, there are special rules. All of these booklets are available free of charge from the Federal Trade Commission. They can also send you a booklet about care labels, and how to design a label, so that all the information is present in the correct format.

Tools

*S*everal types of hand tools and other items must be marked by die-stamping, cast-in-the-mold lettering, etching, engraving or by means of metal plates which are securely attached to the article by welding, screws or rivets. The articles that require these types of markings are:

Cleavers	Surgical instruments
Nippers	Clippers
Dental instruments	Pliers
Forks	Safety Razors
Hinged tools for holding/	Safety razor blades
Splicing wire	Scientific/laboratory instruments
Knives	Scissors
Pincers	Vacuum containers
Shears	and parts of all these
Steels	articles

There are many other special marking requirements – be sure to call Customs to find out if your product is subject to any of them. One phone call is all it takes to avoid disaster.

Exceptions to Marking Requirements

*N*umerous exceptions to the 19 USC 1304 marking law exist, but these exceptions don't apply if special marking is required by some other law (e.g., the special marking for watches and clocks or the FTC marking for apparel).

The first major list of exceptions can be found in section 134.33 of the Customs Regulations. **This section is the J-List. It names 83 specific items that do not have to be marked on the product itself, but allows the packaging to carry the country of origin marking** (See Appendix E-1). The more common articles are works of art, unstrung beads, small ball bearings, bolts, nuts, washers, charcoal briquettes, small buckles, buttons, playing cards, pills, cigarettes, eggs, feathers, hair nets, nails...the list goes on and on. Consult it to see if your product is eligible for this exception.

The "general exceptions" are for things such as items more than twenty years old at the time of importation, goods to be used by the importer and not resold, crude substances, articles that will be further processed in the U.S. and others. If you are importing something that will be manufactured into something else in the U.S., you may be exempt from marking. A complete list of the general exceptions is included as Appendix E-2.

If you qualify for any of the exceptions, chances are the product's container will have to be marked with the country of origin of the product, especially if it is being sold to a retail consumer. Containers themselves have a whole set of marking rules, depending on whether they are "usual" packing, or are "reusable" containers, or if the container imparts the "essential character" to the product.

Containers

"*U*sual" containers are normally sold at retail with their contents. They may be sturdy and reusable (like a wooden cigar box) or may be specially shaped (like a camera case). They do not, as a general rule, need to be marked with their own country of origin unless they are being imported and sold empty. "Usual" containers are almost always classified with their contents. (Classification and duty rates are discussed in another chapter.)

"Reusable" containers may have to be marked separately if they are classified separately from their contents; for example, candy imported in a crystal dish. Since that crystal dish is not a "usual" container for candy at the time of importation, it would be classified separately from the candy, and duty would be paid at a different rate. This dish would have to bear a label with its own country of origin, as well as the country of origin of the candy. Think of it this way – if it's a "separate article of commerce" it has to be marked. Why is the consumer paying $50 for this item – for the candy, or for the dish?

Non-reusable containers are normally discarded after the contents are used up. Whether and how it must be marked depends on whether you are importing it empty to resell as-is, importing it empty to fill it, or importing it with the product in it. You must determine who the "ultimate consumer" is, and whether that person will know where the contents and/or packing were made. This is a complex situation, so you should confer with Customs or a consultant to determine what you have to do.

In a nutshell, if the containers are imported empty for resale as-is they must be marked with their own country of origin in the quantities as sold. For example, if you are reselling paper boxes in bundles of 12, then each bundle must show the country, if each individual box is not marked. See how easy this is?

If the importer is going to fill the containers, they don't need their own country of origin, but the country of origin of the contents will have to be shown.

If they are imported full, the country of origin of the contents must be shown on the container unless it is unsealed and the consumer normally opens the package before buying and the contents are marked. If they are sealed, or are not normally opened prior to sale, then the package must show the country. This is difficult territory and you should always check with Customs ahead of time.

Repacking

*S*ometimes, if an imported item is going to be repacked prior to sale in the U.S., there is a marking exception. This requires that the importer submit to Customs a "repacking certificate." It says that if the repacking conceals or obliterates the marking on the product, the new container will be marked to show the country of origin.

Miscellaneous Headaches

*H*ere is an interesting problem. You believe your product and its container are marked properly. You are so proud of this product that you have your name and address printed right there on the box, in big letters - "AMERICA'S BEST DO-DAD" - Distributed by TEXAS DO-DADS, Dallas, Texas. "Unfortunately, you have overlooked **section 134.46 of the Regulations. It states that whenever a location name, other than the country of origin, appears on an article or its packaging, and that name may mislead or deceive the purchaser as to the actual country of origin, there shall appear"** in close proximity to such words, letters or name, and in at least a comparable size, the name of the country of origin preceded by 'Made In,' 'Product of,' or other words of similar meaning."

The close proximity requirement has been generally interpreted to mean "same side of the box" and "comparable size" means the country of origin has to be in print at least as big as, or larger than, the other location name. This requirement is designed to prevent an importer from misrepresenting the country of origin, or trying to distract the purchaser from the marking. Sometimes if the county of origin is at least as conspicuous as the other location name, it need not be in the same size lettering.

Souvenirs are a little different. How many times have you picked up a souvenir spoon or key chain showing a U.S. location (Beautiful SAN FRANCISCO; Exciting LAS VEGAS) only to turn it over, and find a sticker that says

"Made in Taiwan?" The rule for souvenirs regarding "close proximity" means that it must have its country of origin in a place at least as conspicuous as the U.S. location, even if it's not on the same side of the article.

Some items are assembled in one foreign country from components that are made in the U.S. and other countries. This is a special program which will be discussed in a later chapter. These items are considered to be a product of the foreign country where they are assembled. The importer of the finished product has several marking options:

> **Assembled** in (country of final assembly).

> **Assembled** in (country of final assembly) from components of (countries of origin of all components).

> **Made** in (country of final assembly).

> **Product** of (country of final assembly).

Not Legally Marked - Marking Notice Issued

*T*his notation strikes fear in the hearts of importers and Customs Brokers – "NLM-MNI." This is what the Customs Inspector writes on the invoice when he examines your goods and finds that either there is no marking at all, or the marking is deficient in some way, and he or she is issuing a "marking notice."

A marking notice is a Customs Form 4647 and it should notify you of the problem and the method of correcting it. **You will have 30 days to mark, export or destroy the goods.** Usually, the importer or Customs Broker marks the merchandise as required, or applies for an exception. He certifies the marking notice in the appropriate block and returns it to Customs. Customs can then either accept the certification or verify that the marking has been done. If they accept it, or verify it and everything has been done correctly, they sign off the notice and your shipment may proceed. You also have the option to export or destroy the shipment, but these must be done under Customs supervision, so be sure to check with your Customs Broker before you do either.

Sometimes Customs finds a marking problem at some later date, after the goods have been released to the importer. For example, they may request that you send them a sample from the shipment, instead of examining the goods on the dock. If the sample you send is improperly marked, they can issue a marking notice at that point, within certain time limits, but now it is called a "Demand For Redelivery." **You have 30 days to mark the shipment as required, and Customs almost certainly will want to verify it, so you must have all the goods in that shipment physically available for Customs Officers to review**. This could create quite a problem if you have already sold half (or all) the merchandise. The solution is to make sure the goods are properly marked prior to importation, and do not remove the marking from sales samples you submit to Customs.

Dire Consequences

*I*n cases where foreign merchandise is not legally marked, the LEAST that can happen is that delivery of your shipment will be delayed. This causes problems with your customers, who are eagerly awaiting America's Best Do-Dads.

If a Demand for Redelivery is made, and you don't redeliver, the fine can be as high as the value of the goods plus the duty. This is called "liquidated damages." You are also liable for "marking duties" in the amount of 10% of the value of the shipment. These fines are to discourage importers from (1) importing goods that are not marked and (2) not redelivering them to Customs when requested to do so. Often the excuse is, "Sorry, Customs, I already sold those goods and can't get them back."

If you submit a "false certification of marking" - that is, you sign the marking notice certifying that the goods are marked, and the Inspector comes to your warehouse and

finds that they are NOT marked - the goods are usually seized and trust me, you don't want that to happen. We'll deal with seizures in a later chapter. Customs might also determine that negligence, gross negligence or fraud was involved, and issue a penalty for that, and maybe also a criminal penalty up to $10,000 and five years in jail for the importer who signed the certification.

If the goods are marked when they are imported but some dastardly person removes, alters or defaces the marking later, that person is eligible for a fine of $5,000 and a year in jail. The Customs Service is serious about country of origin marking. Take no chances. **Get a copy of Part 134 of the Customs Regulations (19 USC 1304) and talk to Customs, your Customs Broker or a consultant to stay out of trouble.**

What Do I Need To Do?

Learn the marking requirements for your product and communicate them to the foreign supplier.

Determine who the ultimate consumer is and mark the product in a manner permanent enough so that person will know the country of origin.

Be sure the product was actually made in the country appearing on the marking label.

Determine whether you are eligible for any of the exceptions granted by the Customs Regulations.

If you repack imported goods, or sell to repackers, submit the necessary notifications and certificates to Customs to ascertain whether the marking is acceptable.

Respond promptly to marking notices and demands for redelivery.

DO NOT alter, deface or remove country
of origin marking or sign a false
certification of marking.

References and Resources

Title 19, Code of Federal Regulations, Part 134 (Marking)
U.S. Customs Marking Digest

Harmonized Tariff Schedule of the U.S. - Chapter 91, US
Note 4, Special Marking Requirements for Watches and
Clocks.

The following booklets are available free of charge from the
Federal Trade Commission:
  The Textile Fiber Products Identification Act
  The Fur Products Labeling Act
  The Wool Products Labeling Act
  Fair Packaging and Labeling Act
  How To Design a Care Label

Publications are available from Boskage Commerce Publications, Ltd.
(1-888-880-4088)

Chapter Nine

Other Agency Requirements
It's Not Just for Customs Anymore

Introduction

*W*hen the Customs Service was formed a couple of hundred years ago (in 1789 to be exact), its primary goal was to collect enough money in duties to finance the fledgling government and get the country out of debt. Until the creation of the income tax, Customs duties were virtually the sole source of government revenue.

Money collected as duty on imported merchandise built the first ships of the new Navy, paid for the military academies at West Point and Annapolis, and the building of the city of Washington, DC. Customs duties even financed the Louisiana Purchase. In 1835 the national debt was zero because of collections made by U.S. Customs. In 1975 the national debt could have been retired, if Customs could have collected all the money it was owed. We all know where the national debt has gone since then.

Current duties are now a relatively small percentage of the United States budget, and are used mainly to "level the playing field" for U.S. manufacturers. The main objective for U.S. Customs has become the enforcement of hundreds of laws for the other agencies that have been created during the last 200 years.

Since Customs is the first, and sometimes only, agency available to look at merchandise as it enters the United States, the enforcement responsibility has fallen largely to the Customs Inspector and Import Specialist.

Although Customs enforces these "other agency" laws and can give you basic information about the requirements, you should always contact that other agency for details. Let's talk about a few common products that have "other agency requirements."

Department of Agriculture

*T*hese folks are interested in just about everything that grows out of the ground, and some things that walk upon it. Among other things, Agriculture is tasked with keeping insect and other pests out of the U.S. to the greatest extent possible. Licenses are required for importing various kinds of meat and cheese. Special fees, in addition to Customs duty, are assessed against livestock and cotton products. Many kinds of seed stock and fruits and vegetables must have special permits and inspection certificates. Some animals cannot be imported at all if the exporting country is designated as infected with Foot and Mouth Disease or Newcastle Disease. Even brooms, if they are made with vegetable materials, must pass muster with the Agriculture Department, and containers of baskets must be fumigated to ensure that no insects enter the U.S. illegally, *i.e.*, without little tiny passports.

Department of Commerce

*A*ll statistical information about your shipment – what you bought, how much you paid for it, where you got it – is forwarded electronically by Customs to the Bureau of the Census in the Department of Commerce. These figures are then used to compile trade statistics and are available to the public for the asking. The statistics are used by the government in negotiating trade agreements with other countries.

Textile quotas are administered by Commerce, even though the actual law providing for quotas is a Department of Agriculture agreement.

Commerce also regulates things like automotive products; educational, scientific and cultural materials; and all exports from the United States. Some of this agency's more colorful laws are the Sponge Act (1914); the Tuna Convention Act of 1950 (doesn't this conjure up a vision of several hundred large fish in seminar rooms, listening to speeches?); and a law that prohibits whaling without the appropriate license or permit.

Department of Energy

*V*irtually all petroleum products require licenses to import. If you are going to import oil, it's a good idea to contact a Customs port that sees a lot of these importations, namely Houston, Texas. Calling a port like Dallas or El Paso won't get you the information you need, since the Import Specialists there have never seen a tanker full of crude.

Food and Drug Administration (FDA)

*A*nything you can eat, drink, put on your skin or in your hair, and even a few things you wear (spectacles) or use (therapeutic devices) are within the purview of FDA. Not only do products themselves have to conform to certain standards, but the packages which contain the product have strict rules governing the size and arrangement of information.

If you're thinking of importing dinnerware, FDA is interested. The dishes will have to pass a test governing the amount of lead leaching out of the clay when the dishes are used. Decorative plates, bowls and platters that do not pass this test must be labeled "not for food service" or "for decorative purposes only."

To simplify, anything that might come anywhere near your body will probably be subject to either FDA or CPSC (Consumer Products Safety Commission) rules.

Since September 11, 2001, all government agencies have heightened their enforcement actions to prevent terrorist acts. The FDA and Customs & Border Protection have implemented procedures under the Bioterrorism Act, in order to protect the U.S. consumer from imported food products that may be adulterated with hazardous biological agents.

The main change in procedures has been to require advance notice to Customs and FDA of an arriving shipment. The advance notice time periods vary, depending upon the mode of transportation. For specific details, check the FDA website, www.fda.gov, or Customs at www.cbp.gov. Your Customs Broker will also have up-to-the-minute information as to the reporting requirements.

Consumer Products Safety Commission (CPSC)

The CPSC regulates things that could hurt you that the FDA doesn't handle directly. Children's pajamas must pass a CPSC flammability test, and toys for young children cannot have any small parts that could fall or be pulled off and end up in a little throat. There is actually a special gauge that Customs Inspectors use to determine if a part of a toy is smaller than the minimum. It is a clear plastic tube the size of a three-year-old's windpipe - if the toy part fits in the tube, the toy cannot be imported. There is also a "drop test" that is employed at the time of exam. The Inspector or Import Specialist holds the toy at a designated height, and drops the toy onto a hard surface. If any parts fly off on impact, the toy will either be prohibited, or will have to be labeled for use by certain ages only.

Baby cribs must be constructed to certain specifications to prevent such things as the baby's head being caught between slats, or between the mattress and side. Fireworks are subject to CPSC standards, also, and some require a license from the Bureau of Alcohol, Tobacco, Firearms and Explosives, since they fall into the "explosives" category.

Public Health Service (PHS)

We have numerous agencies protecting our health - FDA, CPSC, EPA and now PHS. Live dogs and cats must be healthy upon entry into this country, and dogs must have a current rabies vaccination. For some reason, cats don't; presumably because cats would never allow themselves to be bitten by a rabid animal.

PHS also requires quarantine of psittacine (parrot-like) birds, and demands permits for other animals. If you are going to import monkeys or other non-human primates, you'll need a permit from the Public Health Service.

Human bodies, if the person died from a quarantinable disease, either have to be embalmed and in a hermetically sealed casket, or cremated. The good news is, no entry is required for a dead body and its accompanying casket and flowers. It just needs to be "declared" to Customs.

Fish and Wildlife Service (FWS)

This agency is interested primarily in non-domesticated animals, and merchandise made from parts of these animals. Any endangered or threatened species, including plants, will probably either need a permit or not be admitted at all. Ivory, which used to be allowed, is now a prohibited importation, unless the importer can prove it is an antique.

Sea turtle boots will probably not make it into the U.S., nor will any animal protected under the Marine Mammal Protection Act of 1972 - polar bears, certain seals and whales. Don't try to import bald eagle feathers unless you are a Native American. Tortoise shell hair ornaments or mirrors, snake skin shoes or purses, anything with feathers on it, bone and shell articles - all require FWS clearance. Also, wildlife products can only be imported at designated ports, so call the Fish and Wildlife Service to be sure the port you want to use is on their list.

Snake skin and fur and tortoise shell look better on their original owners, anyway. Why buy products made with wild animal parts?

State Department

*A*rtifacts and cultural property imported from various countries must have permits from the foreign government. Before you go on an archeological dig, be sure you know what the foreign country is allowing to be exported. If you are going to buy antiquities in a foreign country, my advice is to be an expert in that particular commodity. If you are not, you will either end up buying a fake, or the item you buy cannot leave its country legally. Buy some copies at the local tourist market, instead. That way you won't end up in some south- or central-American jail, or in trouble with U.S. Customs.

The State Department also regulates the export of munitions, so if you're planning on being a defense contractor or gun-runner, you'll want to visit them and find out their requirements.

Department of Transportation (DOT), Environmental Protection Agency (EPA), and the Federal Aviation Administration (FAA)

*T*he most common product regulated by DOT and EPA is automobiles. Cars must meet all the DOT and safety and EPA emissions standards for their make and model year. The

Department of Transportation has safety standards for bicycles, too, and various kinds of tires.

The Environmental Protection Agency also likes to regulate chemicals. You'll need to be familiar with the Toxic Substances Control Act to see if your product falls under its restrictions. Various permits and licenses may be required, and special packaging rules and labeling might apply.

The FAA must approve all aircraft and aircraft parts to ensure they meet all safety specifications.

Bureau of Alcohol, Tobacco, Firearms and Explosives (BATFE)

*T*heir name says it all. You need licenses and/or permits from this agency to import alcoholic beverages of all kinds, firearms and other weaponry, and tobacco products. Wine also has to be cleared by the FDA, but distilled spirits don't. Apparently FDA feels the amount of alcohol in booze will kill any of the harmful organisms they regulate.

Distilled spirits, beer and wine carry an Internal Revenue Tax over and above the regular Customs duty, and it can be hefty. Importing alcoholic beverages is not for the amateur, so you should learn this business from the inside before you strike out on your own.

Firearms are also highly regulated and cannot be imported without a license. You must be a licensed firearms dealer before you can even get an import license. Many types of weapons cannot be imported at all, so this is also not a product for the average wannabe importer.

Tobacco products require, in addition to various permits, special package labeling. You can forget Cuban cigars altogether – all trade with Cuba, or the importation of Cuban products, is currently prohibited. Virtually any Cuban cigar that can be procured in the United States has either been smuggled in (which is illegal) or is made in some other country and re-labeled as Cuban (also illegal). It's a consumer rip-off as well.

Foreign Assets Control (FAC)

*T*he U.S. maintains special trade restrictions for products from Cuba, Iran, North Korea, and others. Foreign Assets Control issues licenses to import products that would otherwise be prohibited (Cuban cigars, Iranian carpets). There are certain exceptions for personal property, and certain cases where you can get an FAC license, but in general, commercial shipments of Persian rugs (and almost everything else from Iran) are prohibited. Don't try to describe them as Turkish or Chinese rugs, either; Customs has experts who can tell the difference.

 The countries subject to restrictions change with the political winds, so watch the newspapers for clues – then call Customs.

Federal Trade Commission (FTC)

*T*he most common products regulated by the FTC are textiles, fur articles, and apparel. You must have these products labeled in particular ways, with particular information, which is discussed in more detail in the chapter about textiles. The FTC will be glad to send you some free brochures - just call them and ask for the Textile Fiber Products Identification Act, the Fur Products Labeling Act, the Wool Products Labeling Act, the Fair Packaging and Labeling Act and, last but not least, How to Design a Care Label. Don't be put off by the titles - these are easy-to-read brochures and are not as intimidating as they sound.

Through Customs laboratory testing, Customs occasionally checks the "fineness" markings on gold and silver products. It is against the law to label something "sterling" if it isn't. If a ring is engraved "14K" it must be 14 carat gold. There is no requirement to mark the fineness of precious metals, but if the marking is there, it must be accurate.

Our daily lives are regulated by the government in ways most people never realize. Customs officers look for much more than illegal drugs when they examine a shipment. These are only a few examples of "other agency requirements."

What Do I Need To Do?

When you call Customs to find out your product's duty rate, ask if it is subject to any other agency's regulations.

Contact the appropriate agency for details about import requirements.

References and Resources

Title 19, Code of Federal Regulations, Parts 10, 11 and 12.

Handbook of Other Agency Requirements - US Customs Handbook number 3000-02.
Title 7, CFR - Agriculture
Title 15, CFR - Commerce and Trade
Title 21, CFR - Food and Drugs
Title 26, CFR - Internal Revenue
Title 27, CFR - Alcohol, Tobacco and Firearms
Title 37, CFR - Patents, Trademarks and Copyrights
Title 40, CFR - Protection of the Environment
Title 50, CFR - Wildlife and Fisheries

Publications are available from Boskage Commerce Publications, Ltd.
(1-888-880-4088)

Chapter Ten

Pre-Entry Rulings

See the Future

Introduction

*I*mporters need to know ahead of time how much their product will cost, so they can establish a markup sufficient to make a profit. Since Customs duty can be a significant cost factor, it is necessary to know the exact amount that will be charged. **The best way to nail down this information is to obtain a binding ruling from the Customs Service.**

Various people within Customs write rulings. The attorneys in Customs Headquarters in Washington, DC specialize in the more complex and controversial issues, such as appraisement, country of origin determinations, marking and issues where there is dis-agreement within Customs. (And there is often such disagreement. There is even an established, formal procedure for "differences" between Field Import Specialists and National Import Specialists.)

The National Import Specialists (NIS) are functionally a part of the Office of Regulations and Rulings in Headquarters. Each NIS handles a very limited portion of the Harmonized Tariff Schedule, so they are the recognized experts in particular commodities. The NIS frequently consult with the Field Import Specialists (FIS) located in the ports regarding classification and value issues. The NIS also conduct training for the FIS in their specific commodity lines. The NIS are the "hub" of the classification rulings program.

Most of the larger Customs ports have commodity specialist teams, each of which consists of several Import Specialists. The typical team might consist of a Team Leader and two or more Import Specialists, and perhaps a few Inspectors. This team configuration is by no means standard throughout Customs. Some ports do not have the resources to assign more than one or two people to a team.

According to recent information from Customs, approximately nine thousand rulings are issued per year, and less than one and a half percent of those need to be modified or revoked later due to an error or change of practice. Most rulings issued by NIS's must be sent to the importer within thirty days of receiving the request.

Obtaining a binding ruling has been listed by Customs as being one way of exercising Mod Act "reasonable care." **Failing to obtain one could just as easily be considered a failure to exercise reasonable care in the event you classify your merchandise incorrectly.**

Binding Rulings

A ruling letter, issued for classification only, can cover up to five items and is issued by Customs well within the 30-day time limit. The importer submits a request for a ruling to a Customs office and it is forwarded to New York for numbering and assignment to the appropriate NIS. A request for a ruling must contain certain information. The request may cover a maximum of five similar items, must concern a prospective shipment, and be submitted in triplicate. The following information must be included in the request:

Names, addresses and other identifying information of all interested parties, if known; the manufacturer ID code, if known.

Name(s) of the port(s) in which the merchandise will be entered, if known.

Description of transaction; for example, a prospective importation of (merchandise) from (country).

A statement that there are, to the importer's knowledge, no issues on the commodity pending before Customs or any court.

A statement as to whether classification advice had previously been sought from a Customs officer; and if so, from whom, and what advice was rendered, if any.

Full and complete description of the article, including what materials it is made of, the percentages/weights of each.

The article's principal use in the U.S.

The commercial, common or technical designation.

Chemical analysis, flow charts, CAS number, etc.

Any special invoicing requirements in part 141 of the Customs Regulations.

Any other pertinent information.

Be certain that your request includes all the necessary information and that the required statements are made (check the Customs Regulations for the most current requirements). If you leave anything out, Customs will either call you or send your letter back, telling you what they need. In this case, the 30-day period starts again when they receive the additional information.

Rulings are binding in all ports, and a copy must be submitted with the entry for the merchandise. They are effective on the date of the ruling letter, and remain in effect until revoked by Customs, or changes in the merchandise render the letter invalid.

Account Management

*C*ustoms has recently implemented a program of "account management" that may impact the Rulings program for some importers.

In the Account Management system, large importers will be assigned to a particular individual within Customs who will handle that importer's entire line of merchandise and all issues that may arise. Your "account" may be handled out of Washington, DC or at a local port.

There would be some advantages to this type of program. Uniformity for the importer would improve, since only one person would be making the Customs decisions. The importer would not have to endure requests for information duplicated in various ports, or repetitive examination of the same product. A rapport could be established between the importer and the Customs account manager.

However, there would be a few disadvantages as well. Could one person acquire enough product expertise to handle the entire Tariff Schedule when the "account" is a large retail chain that imports everything under the sun? Have you ever enjoyed playing phone tag with a person in another city? Will the travel expenses for meetings with your account manager be worth it? Would personnel turnover, both in Customs and in the importer's office, impact the relationship?

Details are sketchy at this point, and few importers are being handled this way as this book goes to press. These issues will undoubtedly have to be resolved one importer at a time.

In conjunction with Account Management, Customs is developing a "Self Governance" system. This is one of many new ideas being explored, so watch the Federal Register and Customs Bulletin (or the Customs website) for information as the test program develops.

Importer Self-Assessment involves a company having a preliminary consultation with Customs (possibly even a Compliance Assessment audit), and implementing strong internal controls to comply with laws and regulations. The company will, in essence, audit itself on a regular basis and report to Customs, either on an annual or transaction basis. Customs will perform limited checks to determine compliance. It is a voluntary program that involves a signed agreement, creating civil and criminal liabilities.

The benefits of Importer Self-Assessment will supposedly be fewer cargo exams, fewer audits, fewer requests for information from Customs and reduced penalty exposure. The downside is that the program is intrusive, expensive and geared to larger importers. There is less attorney-client privilege. If the importer is found to be non-compliant, implementing an improvement plan will be required.

Further information about the Importer Self-Assessment program is available on the Customs website, www.cbp.gov.

Value Rulings

A request for a ruling on the value of goods must be sent to Customs Headquarters in Washington, DC 20229. As in classification rulings, the request must contain a detailed description of the transaction to be considered for the ruling.

At a minimum, for a value ruling, the request should contain:

Names and addresses of all interested parties, foreign and domestic.

Description of the product(s) to be imported.

Port(s) of entry, if known.

Nature of the transaction (e.g., sale, consignment, transfer of property, etc.).

Terms of sale, and the price.

Currency used, and method of conversion to U.S. dollars.

Whether the transaction is between "related parties" and whether or not the relationship affects the price.

Whether buying or selling agents were utilized, and the amounts of their commissions.

Whether any "assists" were provided, the type and value.

Whether identical or similar merchandise is being imported.

Whether any rebates, proceeds of sale or other amounts accrue to the foreign seller after importation into the U.S.

Requesting a value ruling requires some knowledge of the value laws and regulations. You must present Customs with all the pertinent facts so that their ruling will correctly address the situation. If you leave even one significant detail out, it could change the outcome. Chapter Five of this book discusses the basic value concepts of the Trade Agreements Act of 1979, but the importer should also be familiar with the appraisement section of the Customs Regulations, 19 CFR 152.23 through 152.108.

Internal Advice

*I*f your issue or transaction is not prospective in nature, that is, you already have a shipment that is before Customs for classification or appraisement, and you disagree with Customs' position, you may request the field officer to obtain an **Internal Advice. This is, essentially, the field office asking Customs Headquarters to make the decision.**

Usually, it is faster to register your disagreement in the form of a Protest (See Chapter Seven) because an Internal Advice can sometimes languish for years in Washington. Requests for Internal Advice must contain all the information other rulings require, plus any legal basis for your arguments.

Country of Origin Determinations

*T*hese rulings may be requested by a foreign producer, an importer, a U.S. manufacturer or wholesaler of a similar product, a U.S. labor organization or association, or a U.S. trade or business association. The names of interested parties must be included, as well as all pertinent facts. Give a description of the existing article for which the country of origin determination is requested, and the country claimed to be the country of origin.

NAFTA Rulings

*I*f your company does business with customers or suppliers in Canada or Mexico, you will want to know if your product qualifies for the reduced duty provisions under NAFTA. Rulings must be requested from the importing country's Customs department. Only certain issues may be ruled on under Part 181 of the Customs Regulations, for imports into the U.S.:

> **Whether** foreign materials undergo the required tariff shift in the NAFTA territory.
>
> **Whether** a regional value content requirement is met.
>
> **Whether** the producer's method of calculating the regional value content is acceptable.
>
> **Whether** a good qualifies as an "originating good" or is eligible for duty-free treatment when returned after repair or alteration.
>
> **Whether** country of origin marking is acceptable.

These ruling may be requested by importers in the U.S., and exporters in Canada and Mexico. Consult Part 181 of the Customs Regulations for details as to where to submit your request, and the information required.

In General

*I*f you request a ruling, and you disagree with Customs' conclusion, you always have the option of requesting a "reconsideration" or appeal. The procedures vary for each type of ruling, so consult the Customs Regulations for instructions. As a last resort, your position can be litigated in the Court of International Trade.

Customs continually implements new programs involving compliance issues. The prudent importer periodically checks the website to determine the current options available, and reviews the pertinent Informed Compliance publications.

What Do I Need To Do?

Check with an NIS or the Customs Regulations to determine the current procedures for requesting a ruling.

When requesting a ruling, include all pertinent information.

Provide a copy of the ruling to your Customs Broker(s) for use in filing entries.

If you disagree with a port ruling, request review by Customs Headquarters.

References and Resources

Title 19, Code of Federal Regulations
   Part 177 (Administrative Rulings)
   Part 181 (NAFTA).

Publications are available from Boskage Commerce Publications, Ltd.
(1-888-880-4088)

Chapter Eleven

Fraud and Its Consequences

It's Not Nice to Fool Customs

Introduction

*T*he concepts of informed compliance and reasonable care in the Customs Modernization Act assume that most importers are honest and will voluntarily comply with the law. Many Customs employees believe this and treat importers accordingly, in a business-like manner. Some don't . Some officers believe that all importers routinely and intentionally evade laws and those few officers look at everything as a violation that just needs to be exposed. Sometimes it's difficult to distinguish between a routine inquiry, necessary to process your entry, and a more serious investigation.

It is one thing to be visited by an Import Specialist who wants to verify information shown on one of your entries, and perhaps take a tour of your facility to see how your product is made or how you do business. It's quite another to be visited by a Special Agent who is investigating the possibility that you have done something fraudulent. The first situation is routine and is primarily for the education of the Import Specialist, and for developing a rapport with you, the importer. The second situation can be much more serious.

The Special Agent is a Customs officer who is trained in investigative techniques and is the equivalent of a plainclothes detective on a police force. The Agent carries a weapon, occasionally serves search warrants, works in undercover operations, and sees to the prosecution of the bad guys. This officer does not look at routine entry paperwork, classify merchandise or inspect cargo. Most cases handled by the Office of Investigations concern drug and arms smuggling, money laundering and other criminal violations that often make the six o'clock news. However, in recent years, Agents have been participating more and more in cases involving commercial fraud.

 The law that covers Customs fraud is 19 USC 1592. A violation of this law occurs when, "a person, through fraud, gross negligence or negligence, enters, introduces or attempts to enter or introduce any merchandise into the commerce of the United States by means of any document, written or oral statement, or act which is material and false, or any omission which is material; or when a person aids or abets any other person in the entry, introduction or attempted entry, or introduction of merchandise by such means." (19 CFR 177, Appendix B)

The "materiality" of the violation is key. **Under this law, "material" means that the violation has the potential to alter the Harmonized Tariff Schedule classification, value or admissibility of the merchandise, or a person's liability for duty; or it conceals unfair trade practices; or it involves an unfair act concerning copyrights, trademarks or other intellectual property rights.**

An error in classification isn't a 1592 violation if it's an honest mistake or difference of opinion. Something that is deliberately described incorrectly on an invoice to get a lower duty rate is definitely a violation. Stating that an item is made in France, when you know it was made in Taiwan and that the quota for Taiwan is filled, is a material false statement because it affects the admissibility of the goods.

If the importer shows on the entry documents that the country of origin of bearings is Iceland, to conceal the fact that they are really Japanese bearings subject to an Anti Dumping order, it is concealing an unfair trade practice (the dumping). Trying to import counterfeit or piratical copies of the latest best-selling music CD is also a violation of 19 USC 1592.

In order to fall under 19 USC 1592, the falsity or omission must be due to "fraud, gross negligence or negligence." These terms are important because they denote the "level of culpability" which determines the amount of the penalty assessed for the violation.

 "Negligence" is the failure to exercise reasonable care and competence to ensure that a statement made is correct. Another way to express it is, "You should have known better." A reasonable person in the same circumstances would have found out the correct information and avoided the error. If a person has actual knowledge of, or wanton disregard for the facts, or acts with indifference to or disregard for legal obligation, that person is guilty of "gross negligence." The person knew better, but didn't care. It was more expeditious to do it the wrong way.

The highest (or lowest, depending upon your point of view) level of culpability is "fraud." The act is committed knowingly, voluntarily and intentionally. Fraud is the most difficult for Customs to prove, because they must establish intent, through "clear and convincing evidence." If they conduct an investigation of your company, and find a letter in your files instructing the shipper to invoice only half the shipment's value so you'll pay less duty, they have what is known as a smoking gun and could easily establish fraud. Most of the time they're not that lucky.

Penalties

*T*he Customs Regulations contain a somewhat complex penalty system to punish violations of 19 USC 1592. The amount will depend first on the level of culpability. Then they consider whether there was a "prior disclosure" (i.e., a confession) by the importer, and factor in various aggravating and mitigating circumstances, and whether or not there was a loss of revenue (duty). Then they refer to certain formal "mitigation guidelines," do some arithmetic and, presto - arrive at the penalty amount. It only seems like they're picking a number out of a hat after reading chicken bones.

The maximum penalties, when the importer has not made a prior disclosure, are:

For Fraud - the domestic value of the merchandise. (Domestic value is the appraised value, plus freight, insurance, Customs Brokerage fees, duty/entry fees, delivery to the importer's premises, and the importer's usual markup. If the importer is a retailer, the domestic value may be a substantial amount.)

For Gross Negligence - the lesser of the domestic value, or four times the loss of revenue. If there was no loss of revenue, 40% of the dutiable value.

For Negligence - the lesser of the domestic value or two times the loss of revenue. If there was no loss of revenue, 20% of the dutiable value.

If the importer has submitted a valid prior disclosure (discussed later in this chapter) there are virtually no penalties to speak of:

For Fraud - one time the loss of revenue; if no loss of revenue, 10% of the dutiable value.

For Gross Negligence and Negligence - interest on the loss of revenue.

In addition to penalties, Customs can also collect any duty lost, even though liquidation of the entry is final. The statute of limitations under 19 USC 1592 is five years:

For Gross Negligence and Negligence - from the date of the occurrence.

For Fraud - from the date of discovery of the violation.

Fortunately for importers, Customs rarely collects the maximum penalty. If you should be so unfortunate as to receive the dreaded "pre-penalty notice," obtain legal help and file a petition. Never just pay the initial amount Customs designates. There is almost always a chance of reducing the penalty amount.

The "mitigation factors" listed in the Customs Regulations (and this list is not exclusive) are:

> **Contributory Customs Error** - if Customs had given you an opinion or advice that caused you to make the mistake, that is a contributory Customs error.
>
> **Cooperating With the Investigation** - however, merely providing the records Customs asks for is not considered "cooperation justifying mitigation." You must go out of your way to help the investigators.
>
> **Immediate Remedial Action** - paying the duty owed or firing the individual responsible for the "material falsity" may help.
>
> **Inexperience in Importing** - this is only considered a mitigating factor in "negligence" cases. Customs recognizes that import laws are many and complex, and are willing to give new importers a break. One.
>
> **Prior Good Record** - this is considered only in "negligence" or "gross negligence" cases.

There could be other factors that might cause a reduction in a penalty. Circumstances vary so widely from case to case, Customs will look at anything you wish to present. One thing that doesn't work, though - saying your company will go out of business if you have to pay the penalty. If you've been proven guilty of fraud, trust me - Customs doesn't care.

After you've tugged at Customs' heartstrings with your mitigating factors, there are the "aggravating factors."

> **Obstructing** the investigation.
>
> **Withholding** evidence.

Providing misleading information.

Prior violations of 19 USC 1592.

Again, this list is not exclusive. Just remember that law enforcement officers really hate it when laws are violated. Some of them seem to take it personally. You don't want to "aggravate" them any more than they are already!

When all the mitigating and aggravating factors are considered, the Fines, Penalties and Forfeitures folks apply the mitigation guidelines to arrive at an amount. If you want to know the details of those guidelines, see 19 CFR 171, Appendix B(D), Disposition of Cases.

Investigations

*H*ow and why does Customs begin an investigation? Most of the time, commercial fraud cases result when either an Inspector or Import Specialist suspects that an importer is up to some hanky-panky, and refers it to the Office of Investigations. Some ports also have Commercial Fraud Teams, consisting of all the various officers - Import Specialists, Inspectors, Agents and Auditors.

Some cases are generated by informants (disgruntled ex-employees and ex-spouses are good sources for Customs). Other investigations result from analysis of statistical information, or from doing computer trend analysis. A Customs employee out doing the usual family shopping may run across a violation. Or a routine visit to one importer who tells an Import Specialist, "Oh, everybody does this" may spark an inquiry. There are as many causes for investigations as there are laws.

There are various ways Customs employs to obtain information after an investigation has started. They may begin by sending the importer a Request for Information, CBP Form-28. However, this form is used mainly for routine inquiries, and does not usually indicate that Customs has started an investigation. Sometimes a Summons is used, which is more formal. If the Summons is not complied with, the investigating officers will either get a Court Order or a search warrant. If a search warrant is served on your company, it will most likely not be the high point of your business life. Several Agents will go through your records and seize anything that might be evidence of a crime. This can severely hamper your operations. If Customs must resort to a search warrant, you can be sure the investigation will not be completed very soon, because they must review all those records they seized.

 If a Customs Special Agent visits you, you can be fairly sure that a violation has occurred, and it's more than a minor mistake. It's a good time to get your attorney involved, to ensure that legal procedures are followed. Sometimes Agents will try to get information by intimidation or bluffing, without having that Court Order or search warrant in their pocket. Don't let them bully you into incriminating yourself – call your lawyer.

Prior Disclosure

 If **you discover that your company has made a mistake, and you owe Customs significant duty, you can avoid those pesky penalties by submitting a "prior disclosure."** If you submit this information before an investigation is begun by Customs, usually you will be liable for only the duty plus interest. To be valid, a prior disclosure must meet certain criteria:

> **It must be in writing**, to the port director of the port where your entries are filed, or where the violation occurred.
>
> **It must identify** the entries involved, by entry number or time period.
>
> **It must identify** the falsity and describe the circumstances of the violation.
>
> **You must give** the accurate information.
>
> **You must state** that any unknown information will be provided within thirty days.

You must tender the duties due, either with the prior disclosure or within thirty days of being notified by Customs of the amount due.

It must be made "before or without knowledge of the commencement of a formal investigation of that violation."

"Knowledge" of an investigation can be presumed if you are actually notified by Customs that you are the subject of an investigation, or if an Agent contacts you about the violation or requests records. But not all requests for records or information mean there's an investigation going on. If you get a CF-28 Request for Information from an Import Specialist, asking for a sample or a copy of a purchase order, it's probably a routine inquiry. If you get a request for detailed value information, and in-depth questions about your dealings with foreign sellers, there may be something more to it. Review your own records to discover any problem areas.

Audits

*A*udits differ from investigations primarily in the personnel conducting them. Audits are done by accountants, who may or may not be working with Agents on an investigation. An audit may be a part of a fraud case, or it may be a routine, though in-depth, review of the importer's business records. Usually, the report that is prepared at the end of an audit is given to the Import Specialists, who determine if there will be any change (up or down) in the importer's duty liability. Various factors might cause your company to be audited. Some of the most common are:

It's your turn. In 1995, Customs started auditing importers based on the dollar value of their entries for the previous year.

The same informants that refer information to the Office of Investigations.

Related-party transactions, transfer

pricing, any unusual purchasing arrangements, or additional payments to sellers not included on invoices.

Failure to declare assists. See Chapter Five.

Assembly operations in foreign countries.

An Import Specialist sees something that isn't quite right on your entry documentation, and refers it to the auditors.

The audit procedure is fairly straightforward. Customs will notify you, usually at least thirty days in advance, that they will be visiting you. They tell you what they will be looking at, and have a formal "opening conference" to discuss specifics. Then they come to your premises and audit your records, have a "closing conference" and write their report, sending you a copy. See how easy that was? **Before you get your hopes up, know that some audits can take six months or longer. Be prepared to provide work space for the auditors.**

Depending on the type of audit being conducted, they will be looking at the general structure of your company, its relationship and business dealings with suppliers, and what kind of computer system you use if your accounting records are kept electronically. They will check your recordkeeping system, perhaps your internal controls, and detailed information about your import transactions. Usually they will send you a questionnaire in advance, so the routine information is out of the way before they show up on your doorstep.

Customs audits can be as much fun as one conducted by the Internal Revenue Service.

Don't Panic

*T*his chapter was not meant to scare importers. Customs is not poised and ready to pounce on every minor violation or error to make it into a fraud case. Audits and investigations are comparatively rare, considering how many importers there are in this country. If you keep all the records you are required to, and you aren't trying to defraud the government, you should come through an audit relatively

unscathed. **Educate your employees to recognize and correct problems and mistakes before they become fodder for an investigation.** Be sure there is sufficient internal company communication to ensure that Customs correspondence is routed to the responsible person.

What Do I Need To Do?

Implement a Customs compliance program in your company.

Learn the Customs laws and requirements, and train your employees.

Don't be negligent or grossly negligent, and don't commit fraud.

If you find yourself under investigation, call your attorney.

If you receive a penalty notice, call your attorney.

If you submit a prior disclosure, be sure you have found and corrected all errors.

Check the Customs Internet site and review the audit manuals provided.

References and Resources

Title 19, Code of Federal Regulations
    Part 161 (General Enforcement Provisions
    Part 162 (Recordkeeping, Inspection, Search
        and Seizure)
    Part 171 (Fines, Penalties and Forfeitures)

Publications are available from Boskage Commerce Publications, Ltd. (1-888-880-4088)

Chapter Twelve

Importing Textiles
The Fabric of Society

Introduction

*I*f you do any shopping at all, you are probably aware that most wearing apparel is imported from other countries. There is a large markup on these products, making them seem to be very profitable items to import. A sweater knitted in Indonesia might have a Customs invoice value of $4.00 and easily retail in the U.S. for $35.00. But before you rush out and place your order, there are a few things you should know.

One of the most complicated areas of importing, in terms of rules, restrictions and technical requirements, is textiles. To over-simplify the definition of "textile," let's just say these are products made of cloth. They are covered primarily in Section XI and XII of the Harmonized Tariff Schedule (Chapters 50 through 67). There are the textile articles scattered throughout the tariff schedule. Textiles can be made of vegetable fibers (cotton, linen, jute, etc.), man-made fibers (polyester, nylon, rayon, etc.), and fibers derived from animals (silk and wool). Some "fabrics" can even be made of paper or metallic yarns, as well as plastic fibers such as polyethylene. If the product is made of monofilament with a diameter of one millimeter or less, or made of strips five millimeters or less in width, there is a good chance it is a textile. Always check with Customs to be sure.

You must be absolutely positive about whether or not your merchandise is textile because textiles are subject to

quotas and other restrictions. If you do not ascertain the requirements ahead of time, there is a likelihood you will have big – HUGE – problems when the shipment arrives. Many of these problems cannot be fixed, and the goods must be exported or destroyed.

Quotas and Visas

*T*here are about seventy countries with which the United States has special textile trade agreements. Some countries use a special invoice designed for their visa stamp. **The latest list of these countries should be obtained from Customs or the Committee for the Implementation of Textile Agreements (CITA) in the Department of Commerce before you purchase goods overseas.** Textile merchandise purchased in these countries is subject to quotas or visa requirements, or both.

It's difficult to write a book about quotas and visas because the merchandise covered is different for each country, and new countries are constantly being added to the list. Most Pacific Rim countries are on the list (Taiwan, China, Japan, Malaysia, Indonesia, India, etc.) as well as some Central and South American countries (Brazil, El Salvador, Costa Rica, etc.). In short, almost all countries that can produce quantities of clothing very cheaply are on the list. Most European countries are not subject to the restrictions, but a few are, so check with Customs.

A textile "visa" is a license of sorts that is issued by the producing country. It is a stamp or decal that contains certain information specific to the shipment, and it is usually stamped directly on the commercial invoice prior to exportation from the foreign country. Some countries use a special invoice designed for their visa stamp. Your supplier must get this document. The merchandise cannot enter the United States without the visa, if one is required for the particular product from that country. Your chances of obtaining a visa after the goods arrive in the U.S. are "slim" to "none." In rare cases when the visa is lost by the carrier, the Embassy of that foreign government may be willing to issue a "visa waiver" but this happens infrequently.

Most textile goods from the seventy or so countries are also subject to absolute quota. This means only a specified number of a certain product can enter the United States from that country during the quota period, usually one year. The quota year for most countries is January through December, but some are different. As an example, the bilateral agreement between Taiwan and the United States might say that 3,000,000 dozen pairs of women's cotton denim jeans can be exported from Taiwan and entered into the United States. As entries are filed for this product, the Customs computer deducts (on a first-come, first-served basis) the entered quantities from the total allowed. When the quota amount is reached, no more women's cotton denim jeans from Taiwan may be imported.

Since some foreign countries do not stop exporting when their quota limits have been reached, it is very possible that an importer can buy goods which cannot be admitted into the United States. If a shipment arrives here, and the quota has already "filled," the importer has the option of exporting or destroying the merchandise, or entering it into a Foreign Trade Zone (FTZ) or bonded warehouse. If the goods are put into the FTZ or warehouse, they may not be withdrawn for consumption in the U.S. until the beginning of the next quota period. This can be very costly to the importer in terms of storage charges or lost sales, especially if the quota fills early in the quota year. **If you call Customs and tell the Import Specialist what you will be importing, they can check their records and let you know how close the quota is to being filled.** The information is also available from the Office of Textiles and Apparel in the Department of Commerce, in Washington, D.C. and on the internet.

Some quotas fill on the opening day, and don't re-open until a year later. In these cases, you must present your entry by a specific time on opening day. Then the computer does some fancy arithmetic to determine what percentage of your shipment can be released. Every importer who presents a correct entry at the specified time on opening day gets the same percentage of their shipment, so everyone gets at least part of what they entered. The balance must be exported, destroyed, or put into a Foreign Trade Zone or warehouse.

 I cannot emphasize enough that you must find out ahead of time what type of visa you need, if any, and whether the quota is close to filling. Customs does not have the authority to waive the visa requirement, or let your merchandise in if the quota has filled. If the visa you did get is faulty in some way, it will be considered invalid and rejected.

Some common reasons for deficient visas are:

> **The category number** on the visa is incorrect. Each type of product has a specific category number, found in the HTSUS. For example, cotton woven denim jeans for women are category 348.

> **The quantity shown** on the visa is less than the quantity in the shipment. Usually this error occurs when the quantity is based on the weight. If the visa shows "5,000 KG" but the goods actually weigh 6,000 KG, the visa is invalid and the importer must get a corrected one.

> **The visa is counterfeit.** Customs officers are good at spotting these, and now many countries' visas are electronically transmitted, so duplicate numbers are easily detected.

> **The visa was issued** for the wrong year. Sometimes the visa is issued at the end of the quota year, say, December 29, but for some reason the merchandise isn't exported until the next year, perhaps January 3. This invalidates the visa, because it has to be issued based on the date of export from the foreign country.

Preclude a "bad visa" problem by finding out what category number applies, and investigating the reputation of your supplier. Remember, it's the importer who suffers if there is a mistake.

Special Marking Requirements

*I*f the quota and visa situation isn't enough to discourage you from importing textiles, the Federal Trade Commission has special marking rules for you to follow. You will definitely need to obtain the brochures mentioned in Chapter Eight and at the end of this chapter. There are not only many rules, but many exceptions as well. In general, items which are subject to special marking requirements are:

Wearing apparel.
Handkerchiefs.
Scarves.
Bedding.
Curtains and casements.
Draperies.
Tablecloths, napkins throws.
Floor coverings.
Towels.
Wash cloths and dish cloths.
Ironing board covers and pads.
Umbrellas and parasols.
Batts.
Certain flags.
Cushions
Fibers, yarns and fabrics.
Slip covers.
Afghans and doilies.
Sleeping bags.
Antimacassars and tidies.
Hammocks.
Dresser and furniture scarves.

Some of the items that do not need to comply with the special marking requirements are:

Belts, suspenders, garters.
Permanently knotted neckties.
Shoe laces.
Coated fabrics.
Secondhand articles.
Disposable, non-woven items.
Products for the U.S. military departments.
Upholstery stuffing and outer coverings of

furniture, mattresses and box springs.
Linings, interlinings, filling or padding,
incorporated for structural purposes and not
for warmth.
Stiffenings, trimmings, facings or
interfacings.
Backings, paddings or cushions for floor
coverings.
Sewing and handicraft threads.
Bandages.
Shoes and other footwear.
Headwear, handbags, luggage, lampshades,
toys.

These are a few of the more common items subject to the Textile Fiber Products Identification Act. Check with the Federal Trade Commission to ascertain the requirements for your product.

Items listed above which do have to show the special markings must have a conspicuous label which states the country of origin, the fiber content and the name or "RN" number of the manufacturer, importer or other distributor of the product. The "RN" number is issued by the Federal Trade Commission upon application by the importer.

The textile labeling rules are somewhat complex, but generally, all the information must be in English and there should be no abbreviations except authorized ones. The fiber content must be shown in generic terms (for example, "acrylic" instead of the brand name "Orlon"). If there is less than five percent by weight of a fiber, it must be shown as "other fiber" rather than by name. The labels showing the country of origin, fiber content and name/RN number, must be in a conspicuous place. If you are importing apparel, the best location for this label is in the neck (in upper-body garments) or waistband (in lower-body garments).

There are rules concerning the use of footnotes and ditto marks on labels, as well as animal names, and the term "100%" or "All." The brochures available from the Federal Trade Commission discuss each rule in depth, and give examples of labels for your guidance. **Don't import textiles without becoming familiar with the FTC requirements.**

Classification of Wearing Apparel

*O*btaining a duty rate for clothing can be a challenge. If you call Customs to ask for a non-binding opinion as to the classification, duty rate and quota/visa category for your product, be prepared to provide the following information:

Is the garment knit or woven?

What is the item - blouse, dress, trousers, sweater, coat?

Is the garment for men, women, boys, girls or babies? Or is it unisex? If a shirt buttons left-over-right, it will be considered men's. If it is for a child 86 centimeters or less in height, it is classified as "babies'."

What is the fiber content? Get the percentages from your supplier before you call Customs. The duty rates vary from 4% to 34%, so a "ballpark figure" won't do you much good (check the latest edition of the HTSUS for the current duty rates).

Is the garment being imported as part of a set?

If it is a knit top, what is the number of stitches per inch or per centimeter)? Depending on the stitch count, you could have a shirt, a sweater, a pullover, or an "other" garment. If it is a tee shirt, Customs will need to know the weight of the fabric in grams per square meter.

Is the fabric coated with rubber or plastics? Is it a non-woven, such as felt? Is it waterproof or water-resistant?

If you are importing gloves, are they specifically designed for sports? Do they have fourchettes? Are they looped pile, jersey, lisle?

If your garments are not knit, are they denim? Corduroy? Hand-loomed? Yarn-dyed or piece-dyed? Two or more colors in the warp and/or the filling?

If you don't have the answers to the above questions, contact the manufacturer to get the specifics of your shipment. If you don't know what some of the terms mean (knit, woven, fourchettes, jersey, warp) you should probably work in the garment industry for a while, before starting to import apparel. Or, as usual, send a sample of your product to Customs, and ask for a binding ruling.

What Do I Need To Do?

Get as much information as possible about the product from your supplier.

Call Customs and ask about quota and visa restrictions.

Be sure your supplier can obtain the necessary legal visa and quota for your shipment.

Know the marking requirements for the product you plan to import.

References and Resources

Harmonized Tariff Schedules of the United States - Section XI and XII

Textile Fiber Products Identification Act, Fur Products Labeling Act, Wool Products Labeling Act - brochures available free of charge from the Federal Trade Commission.

Title 19, Code of Federal Regulations - Part 132 (Quotas)

Publications are available from Boskage Commerce Publications, Ltd. (1-888-880-4088)

Chapter Thirteen

Other Special Programs

It's Bound To Be Free From Somewhere

Introduction

*A*lthough United States duty rates for most products are fairly low, there are numerous treaties and agreements that allow merchandise to be imported free of duty. Most of the special programs are designed to encourage manufacturing in developing countries. If the country meets all the requirements of the special program, the duty rate is either reduced, or "free" and other trade barriers such as quotas may be removed.

Generalized System of Preferences (GSP)

*T*his is the most wide-spread trade agreement, covering more than 150 countries. It's been in effect since the mid-1970's and has officially expired several times, only to be renewed by Congress. Some countries that were originally eligible for GSP have been removed from the agreement because they are now considered "developed" and no longer in need of the duty-free incentives. Taiwan, Hong Kong and South Korea are the most notable examples. **The list of currently-eligible GSP countries can be found in the Harmonized Tariff Schedules, General Note 4.** The list of countries shown in the 2005 HTSUS is reproduced in Appendix F.

To qualify for treatment under the GSP, the product being imported into the United States must be grown, produced or manufactured in the beneficiary country (one or more of the countries on the list). It must be shipped directly to the U.S. from the beneficiary country, and not enter the commerce of any other country. Merely packing an article, or diluting something with water, or combining ingredients in a beneficiary country usually will not confer origin, and will not qualify it for the duty-free treatment.

The last requirement is that at least 35% of the product's appraised value (i.e., U.S. Customs value) must have been added in the beneficiary country. For example, if the appraised value of a shipment of widgets is $10,000, at least $3,500 of that value must have occurred in the GSP country. If the widget's parts were made in a third country – Japan, perhaps - and they were assembled in Malaysia, the Malaysian producer would have to provide evidence that the assembly created a new product, and the value added in Malaysia was at least $3,500.

In previous years, the U.S. importer was required to obtain from the producer a Certificate of Origin, "Form A" to qualify for duty-free entry into the U.S. However, use of the Form A was discontinued several years ago, and it may or may not be accepted now as proof of eligibility. **U. S. Customs is currently asking for the actual manufacturing figures from the producer to support the 35% requirement.** The importer must obtain this information if requested by Customs.

U.S.-Israel Free Trade Agreement (IFTA)

*T*he requirements under this treaty with Israel are virtually the same as for GSP. The goods must be the growth, product or manufacture of Israel, with value added of 35% of the appraised value, shipped direct from Israel to the United

States. Packing, diluting or combining does not qualify the product for the duty-free treatment.

The one provision in IFTA that GSP does not have is that the Israel-made product may have U.S. content of up to 15% of the appraised value. This U.S. content can be counted as qualifying content. To illustrate, if your widgets have an appraised value of $10,000, you know that $3,500 is the "qualifying" amount for IFTA eligibility. Let's say the manufacturer in Israel bought materials from France, made the widgets in Israel and his costs were:

Materials (France)	-	$7,900
Labor, etc. (Israel)	-	$2,100
Appraised value	-	$10,000

The product would not qualify for IFTA or GSP. However, if the Israeli manufacturer bought some of the materials from U.S. suppliers, that cost could be counted toward the qualifying content:

materials made in France		$6,500
materials made in U.S.	$1,400	
labor, etc. in Israel -	$2,100	
qualifying content -	$3,500	$3,500
appraised value		$10,000

Now the widgets would qualify for the duty-free treatment under IFTA, although not under GSP, since GSP does not allow U.S. content to be counted in the 35% figure. Israel is also on the GSP list, so it's important to be aware of this U.S. content provision in IFTA. The product may not qualify under GSP, but if there was U.S. content, it may very well be duty-free under IFTA.

Caribbean Basin Initiative (CBI)

*T*he countries eligible for this program as of 2005 are:

Antigua & Barbuda	Haiti
Aruba	Honduras
Bahamas	Jamaica
Barbados	Montserrat
Belize	Netherlands Antilles
Costa Rica	Nicaragua
Dominica	Panama
Dominican Republic	St. Kits & Nevis
El Salvador	Saint Lucia
Grenada	Saint Vincent and the Grenadines
Guatemala	Trinidad & Tobago
Guyana	Virgin Islands, British

Check the latest edition of the HTSUS for the countries currently eligible.

Again, the requirements are similar to GSP's: growth, product or manufacture of one or more of the beneficiary countries; 35% of the value added there; packing, diluting and combining don't qualify the product; and it must be shipped directly to the United States from the CBI country. In addition, U.S. content may be counted up to 15% of the appraised value, as in the Israel Free Trade Agreement. One additional provision makes it even easier for the product to qualify for CBI treatment. If there is any Puerto Rican or U.S. Virgin Island content, the total value of that content may be counted as CBI content.

Numerous products are specifically excluded from CBI eligibility, so be sure to check the list in the Harmonized Tariff Schedule.

Andean Trade Preference Act (ATPA)

*T*he ATPA (not to be confused with APTA, the Automotive Products Trade Agreement) covers Peru, Bolivia, Ecuador and Colombia. The list of requirements is familiar by now:

growth, product or manufacture of the beneficiary country; 35% value added; packing, diluting or combining is not qualifying; direct shipment; U.S. content up to 15% of the value; all U.S., Virgin Island, or Puerto Rican content is eligible. In addition, if there is any content from a CBI country, all of that content can be counted to make the 35% minimum. Please note, however, that ATPA content cannot be counted toward CBI eligibility. Be aware of the excluded products shown in the Harmonized Tariff Schedules.

Compact of Freely Associated States Act (FAS)

*T*his agreement covers the Marshall Islands, Micronesia and Palau. It's not a widely used agreement because there is not very much manufacturing going on in these small island groups. The requirements are similar to GSP: the usual growth, product or manufacture requirement; 35% added value; shipped direct; and U.S. content counted. The exclusions are shown in the HTSUS.

Other Trade Agreements and Treaties

Beginning around the year 2000, the United States negotiated numerous new free trade agreements with a diverse group of countries. Some are patterned after the Generalized System of Preferences, and others bear an uncanny resemblance to NAFTA.

 The African Growth and Opportunity Act (AGOA) covers sub-Saharan countries, i.e., countries mostly located south of the Sahara Desert area. There are some exceptions, so check the HTSUS General Notes. The provisions are similar to GSP in that the product must be the "growth, product or manufacture" of a beneficiary country and 35% of the value must have occurred in AGOA countries. Mere combining, packing or dilution with water does not confer eligibility. Goods must also be imported directly to the United States without entering the commerce of another country. In AGOA, materials made in the U.S. may be counted toward the eligible value, up to 15% of the total value of the finished good.

 The U.S.-Jordan Free Trade Area Implementation Act (JFTA) requires the same 35% qualifying value as the other agreements, as well as the "shipped directly to the U.S." rule, and the exclusion for packing, dilution or combining operations. There are special rules for textiles, as well as some exceptions, so be sure to check the HTSUS General Notes for details.

 The United States liked NAFTA's format so much, the agreements with Singapore, Chile and Australia are very similar. There are lists of products considered to be "wholly originating" and a system of "tariff change" rules of origin. Regional Value Content is another way to qualify your goods under these agreements. There are numerous exceptions (as in NAFTA) so check out those HTSUS General Notes! One difference between NAFTA and these three treaties is the de minimis amount - foreign content that may be disregarded when calculating Regional Value Content or tariff shifts. Under the Singapore, Chile and Australia rules, the de minimis amount is 10% of the value, as opposed to 7% under NAFTA.

Civil Aircraft

*C*ertain products are designated throughout the HTSUS as eligible for duty-free treatment under the Agreement on Trade in Civil Aircraft. "Civil aircraft" is defined as "all aircraft other than aircraft purchased for use by the Department of Defense or the United States Coast Guard." Parts are also eligible for this program. If you decide you want to import a Harrier jet fighter for use in your commute to work (to avoid all that ugly freeway traffic), you can enter it duty-free, as long as you have the proper certification.

The certification may be submitted with each Entry Summary, or once a year as a "blanket" certification to cover all shipments in that year, or when Customs requests it. **The complete text of the certification can be found in the Customs Regulations, in Part 10.183,** but basically the importer states that the aircraft or parts are being imported for use as civil aircraft and have been approved for use as (or in) civil aircraft by the Federal Aviation Administration or the airworthiness authority in the country of exportation. Be sure to take the missiles off the plane before you import it, however, or you'll run afoul of the State Department and the Bureau of Alcohol, Tobacco and Firearms.

Pharmaceutical Products and Chemicals For Dyes

*T*he Harmonized Tariff Schedules designate specific commodities that are duty-free if (1) they are listed in the appropriate chemical appendix to the tariff schedule, and (2) they are imported from a country eligible for Column 1 duty rates. If you are in the chemical business, you probably already know what is covered. There is some classifying and cross-referencing to be done, however, so consulting a Customs chemical expert would be advisable.

This chapter is a very brief outline of the requirements under these special programs. Your situation may be complicated by a number of variables. If you are "related" to your supplier in the beneficiary country, it may impact the value of not only the imported product, but also the materials used to make it. Mere assembly of parts made in other countries may not cause the required "substantial transformation" into a new product, so ensure that enough manufacturing is done to qualify your articles.

Keep in mind also, that not all products from all beneficiary countries are covered by the agreements. The items that do have special duty rates are designated in the "Special" column in the HTSUS, with a Special Program Indicator:

A = Generalized System of Preferences (GSP)

B = Automotive Products Trade Act

AU =	United States-Australia Free Trade Agreement
C =	Agreement on Trade in Civil Aircraft
CA =	North American Free Trade Agreement Goods of Canada, under the terms of GN12
CL =	United States-Chile Free Trade Agreement
D =	African Growth and Opportunity Act
E =	Caribbean Basin Initiative (CBI)
IL =	Israel Free Trade Agreement
J =	Andean Trade Preference Agreement (ATPA)
JO =	United States-Jordan Free Trade Area Implementation Act
K =	Agreement on Trade in Pharmaceutical Products
L =	Uruguay Round Concessions on Intermediate Chemicals for Dyes
MX=	North American Free Trade Agreement Goods of Mexico, under the terms of GN12
R =	United States-Caribbean Basin Trade Partnership Act
SG =	United States-Singapore Free Trade Agreement

If any of these letters are followed by an asterisk (*) it means that there are some exclusions for that tariff number, and you must refer to the General Notes of the HTSUS for further information.

The other major special program is the North American Free Trade Agreement (NAFTA), covering trade between the United States, Mexico and Canada. The provisions and requirements of this agreement are so extensive, it is covered separately in another chapter.

What Do I Need To Do?

When you decide what country will manufacture your product, talk to a Customs Broker or consultant to determine whether it qualifies for a special trade agreement duty rate.

Work with your supplier to obtain all necessary supporting documentation.

Keep up with changes to the programs applicable to your products. Articles and countries are periodically removed from the "eligible" lists and become dutiable.

Review your entries soon after filing to be sure special duty rates are claimed as appropriate. You usually have only 90 days after liquidation to correct an error here.

References and Resources

Harmonized Tariff Schedules of the U.S. - General Notes

Title 19, Code of Federal Regulations - Part 10 (Articles Conditionally Free, Subject to a Reduced Duty Rate, etc.)

Publications are available from Boskage Commerce Publications, Ltd. (1-888-880-4088)

Chapter Fourteen

Intellectual Property Rights

Side-Step the Knock-Offs

Introduction

*I*mporting counterfeit goods into the United States can have serious consequences, not only for the trademark or copyright or patent owner, but also for the consumer. Baby shampoo in a counterfeit-design bottle could cause injury to a child's skin and eyes. An engine might fall off an airplane because the Grade Eight bolts holding the engine to the wing were not actually manufactured to the standards of Grade Eights.

Sometimes a counterfeit is obvious. No one really expects to buy a genuine Rolex watch on a street corner for twenty-five dollars. Similarly, you will not find genuine Dooney and Bourke handbags for sale from the trunk of somebody's car or at flea markets at the bargain price of $29.95. But sometimes, the fact that something is counterfeit isn't readily apparent. Counterfeit Grade Eight bolts carry the die-stamped designation, but can only be detected through laboratory testing.

Among its many responsibilities, U.S. Customs is tasked with enforcing the laws governing the importation of goods covered by copyrights, trademarks and patents. In recent years, the umbrella of intellectual property rights has been expanded to include trade dress (packaging), mask works (computer chip design) and trade names. If your trademark, name or other work is registered with either the U.S. Patent and Trademark Office or the Copyright Office, Library of Congress, you may also register it with Customs so they can deny entry to infringing articles.

Trademarks

A **trademark is a design, word, phrase, logo, etc., that identifies the product as being made by a particular company.** The word "Nike" is a trademark, as is "Coke" or the alligator on Izod shirts. Trademarks are used by the consumer to identify products they want to buy. When people look for a particular trademark, there is a perception of quality, and therein lies the reason for counterfeit, or "knock-off" goods. The counterfeiter can produce the article much more cheaply than the genuine goods, sell it for the same price (or less) and make a large profit. This may hurt sales of the genuine article and, if the counterfeit is of inferior quality (which it almost always is) can damage the reputation of the genuine product. Therefore, trademark owners are very concerned about the importation of these knock-offs.

In order to register a trademark with Customs, it must first be registered with the U.S. Patent and Trademark Office. Then an application is submitted to Customs with the following information:

> **Name, address and citizenship** of the trademark owner.

> **Places of manufacture** of the genuine trademarked goods.

> **Names and addresses** of all foreign entities licensed or authorized to use the trademark.

> **Any foreign parent** or subsidiary company which uses the trademark abroad.

Along with the application you must submit several copies of the certificate of registration from the Patent and Trademark Office, and a registration fee ($190 in 2005) for each trademark being registered with Customs.

Once the trademark is registered with Customs, all ports are notified and the information is added to the computer database. When a Customs officer examines a shipment, the database can be queried to see if any mark observed on the imported goods is registered. If an infringing item is discovered, procedures are in place to investigate, notify the trademark owner, and deny entry or seize the illegal shipment. Customs will continue to provide this protection for the 20-year registration period, or as long as it is renewed. The fee to renew or make changes to the original recordation is $80 (2005).

There are time limits for renewing a recordation and if those deadlines are missed, the applicant must start over again as if it were an original registration. **The renewal request must be submitted within three months after the date of expiration of the current registration.**

If you want to import articles with a trademark, find out who the owner is, and whether importation or use of the mark is restricted to licensees. If you want to protect your own trademark, consult your attorney to pursue the recordation and registration for you. It's a complicated process and should be handled by an expert in the field.

Copyrights

A **copyright is issued for the "expression of an idea."** It can be writing, a fabric design, a toy, a video game, or any number of other products. If a product design is copyrighted, it's a little harder for Customs to detect an infringing article, because they must compare the suspect item to a genuine one (or a picture) to make the determination. Even then, it is usually left to the copyright owner to decide whether the imported good is an infringement.

Your copyright must be recorded at the U.S. Copyright Office, Library of Congress, before it can be protected by U.S. Customs. The procedure is similar to the registration of trademarks. You must apply in writing to Customs Headquarters, and include:

The name and address of the copyright owner.

A statement regarding actual or potential injury from infringing goods.

The country of origin of the genuine articles.

Names and addresses of licensees.

The name of the performing artist, if applicable.

A copy of the Certificate of Registration must accompany the application, along with the fee (($190 in 1998) and five copies of the copyrighted work (except books, magazines, etc., which can be identified by title and author). Photos can also be provided. Customs registration lasts for twenty years, or until ownership of the copyright expires.

Any renewal of copyright registration must occur three months before the expiration of the current registration.

Trade Names

*P*rotection of your company's trade name can be accomplished without recording it with the Patent/Trademark or Copyright Offices. It can be registered directly with Customs using the same procedure, and for the same fee, as registering a trademark or copyright. The information that must be provided is:

The name and address of the owner of the trade name.

The name to be recorded.

Foreign entities authorized to use the name.

A description of goods using the name.

Statements by the owner and two other parties to the effect that the name has been used for at least six months, it is a unique name, and the applicant has the exclusive right to use the name.

Customs will enforce a trade name recordation for as long as the name is in use.

Patents

 A **patent is issued on a new invention, product or process.** Some familiar patents cover machines (calculators), kitchen gadgets (Chip Clip) and new drugs. Other patents protect new hybrid plants (roses) or production methods (acid washing of jeans). Because the patent may not apply to the imported product itself, patents are handled a little differently from copyrights and trademarks.

First, you must record your patent with the U.S. Trademark and Patent Office, but you cannot register it with Customs yet. In order for Customs to exclude merchandise from the United States based on a patent, there must be an Exclusion Order from the International Trade Commission (ITC).

 If a patent owner suspects that foreign goods are infringing the patent, he or she must first apply for a Patent Survey. This application goes to the Commissioner of Customs and contains the name and address of the patent owner, a description of the suspected infringing merchandise, a copy of the patent registration, and the appropriate fee, depending on the length of the survey requested.

The Patent Survey instructions are sent to all Customs ports, and during the survey period, they will report all shipments of suspected infringing goods to the patent owner. They do not detain these shipments, or prohibit entry at this point. After the survey is completed, the ITC investigates, and if the goods are determined to be infringing, issues an Exclusion Order. From that point on, Customs will deny entry to any infringing shipment they discover, and the importer and patent owner can duke it out in court.

Sometimes Exclusion Orders are easy for Customs to enforce, because the patented item can be compared to the imported article and a knock-off is obvious. But with other articles (acid-washed jeans, for instance) a laboratory analysis is necessary. Also, in order to catch an infringing article (trademark, copyright, patent or any other form of intellectual property) the shipment must be examined by Customs, a somewhat rare occurrence.

Trade Dress, Strong Marks and Mask Works

*T*here is nothing in the Customs Regulations about "trade dress." This is the term given to distinctive packaging used on trademarked or copyrighted merchandise. For example, the box of yellow and white stripes you see across the room in the department store is instantly recognizable as a "Giorgio" fragrance, even though you can't see the name. Some trade dress is itself copyrighted, but usually Customs uses the "familiarity" concept to decide whether to detain a shipment. If Customs finds an importation of cologne, regardless of the name, in a Giorgio look-alike box, it will (at the very least) be detained while the copyright-trademark-trade dress issue is investigated.

In recording trademarks with Customs, it is necessary to state on what products the trademark will be used. A hypothetical example would be if the owners of a new trademark register the name "Apollo" for use on athletic shoes and apparel (T-shirts and jackets). "Apollo" becomes the running shoe of choice, and the name becomes world-famous through its TV and print ads and celebrity athlete endorsements. An unrelated importer decides to cash in on the "Apollo" name and puts it on his shipment of sunglasses, because the Apollo Company didn't include that line of merchandise in their recordation. However, under the "strong mark" theory, the shipment can be denied entry or seized because the use of a famous name will mislead the consumer into thinking the trademark owner manufactured the product. This may not happen in a case where the products are not in the same "class" of merchandise.

"Apollo" is famous for sports footwear and clothing, and sunglasses are within the realm of apparel accessories; but if the name "Apollo" was used on a cathode-ray oscilloscope, it would not be considered infringing.

 A "mask work" is defined as "the design of an electrical circuit, the pattern of which is transferred and fixed in a semi-conductor chip during the manufacturing process." (U.S. Customs Publication #549 - "U.S. Customs and Protection of Intellectual Property Rights) In order to protect the copyright of a mask work, the owner must obtain either a Court Order or an ITC Exclusion Order.

Violations

*W*hen Customs discovers an imported article that appears to infringe any recordations or registrations, there are various consequences, depending on the actual violation. The product might be an out-and-out counterfeit, or perhaps only "confusingly similar." Usually, the first step taken by Customs is to detain the shipment. Depending on the circumstances, the goods may be seized or destroyed, or the importer may be able to cut a deal with the copyright or trademark owner to pay a royalty for the right to import the violative merchandise. The copyright or trademark owner may be required to post a bond so that Customs can detain the shipment at no risk to the U.S. Government. In some cases, Customs may permit the offending trademark to be removed prior to release of the shipment. The individual circumstances will dictate the action taken.

It only takes one phone call to Customs to determine if a mark or item is registered and protected under intellectual property rights laws. Find out ahead of time, and avoid any questionable transactions.

What Do I Need To Do?

If you are the owner of a copyright, trademark or other intellectual property, explore the options to protect it from the importation of infringing articles.

If you are an importer, check with Customs ahead of time to ascertain whether there are any IPR issues.

If you are importing copyrighted or trademarked articles, work out a licensing agreement ahead of time so your shipment is not delayed.

References and Resources

Title 19, Code of Federal Regulations
Part 133 (Trademarks, trade names and copyrights)
Section 12.39 (Patents)

Publications are available from Boskage Commerce Publications, Ltd.
(1-888-880-4088)

Chapter Fifteen

Less Common Laws and Provisions

Esoterica

Introduction

*C*ustoms is probably the most complex agency in the federal government. It enforces some 600 laws for 60 different agencies, including state governments. This book covers only a small fraction of the laws, regulations and procedures within Customs' purview, so you should consult with your Customs Broker, attorney or other expert – or Customs itself – to find out what laws and regulations pertain to your situation. Here are a few more laws and programs covered by the Customs Regulations and Tariff Schedule.

Anti-Dumping and Countervailing Duties

*W*hen products are sold to the United States for less than they are sold for in their home market, or less than it costs to manufacture them, it's called "dumping." Why would anyone sell a product at such a loss? Essentially, an article is "dumped" in order to drive the competition in that country out of business, corner the market and then raise the price to regain the money lost during the dumping phase. This has happened in the U.S. with televisions, bearings, integrated circuits and a host of other foreign products.

If a foreign government subsidizes a particular industry through cash grants, bounties or other means, that industry can manufacture its products more cheaply than its U.S. competitors, and sell them at a much lower price. The foreign producer obtains an unfair advantage as a result of the government's subsidy. This is a countervailing duty situation.

 To counteract dumping and foreign governmental subsidies, a domestic (U.S.) industry can file a complaint with the International Trade Administration (ITA). To tremendously oversimplify the process, the ITA conducts an investigation, and if it is established that injury to the U.S. industry is being caused by the dumping or subsidy, additional duty amounts are ordered to "level the playing field" for U.S. producers competing with imports.

The "anti-dumping duty" amounts are specific to foreign manufacturers, and there may be several different rates for the same product from the same country. "Countervailing duties" are industry-wide, so the same rate will be paid, no matter who the foreign producer is. These are both additional amounts, over and above the regular duty amounts, and some can be significant. When I handled food products as an Import Specialist, pistachio nuts from Iran could be imported, but the dumping duty rate was 105 percent of the value. One of the questions you should ask Customs before you import, is "Does my product carry any dumping or countervailing duties?" The dumping and countervailing duty cases being handled by the International Trade Administration take several years to complete, so your entry may not be liquidated for up to four years after the merchandise has entered.

You may get a bill at the end of those four years for more duty than you deposited originally. Occasionally, refunds are issued.

Drawback

 *I*f you import an item, pay duty on it, and then export it, there is a good chance you can get almost all of that duty back from Customs, using the drawback program. This is another area of Customs law that is very complex, so you should hire an expert to advise you.

The three most common types of drawback are "same condition" (or unused), "manufacturing," and "non-conforming merchandise." **In the "same condition" category, the goods being exported from the U.S. are in the same condition as when they were imported, or have** **not been used in the United States. In "manufacturing" drawback, you can import a part, for example, use it in the manufacture of a machine, export the machine and get the duty back that you paid on the part.** To make things interesting, both "same condition" and "manufacturing" drawback allow substitution of goods, so it is not necessary to export the same thing you imported originally. In some cases, you can claim drawback and get the duty refund even if you weren't the importer who paid the duty in the first place. See why you need an expert?

 If you imported goods that did not conform to sample or your specifications, you can return them to the foreign supplier and get a duty refund from Customs under "non-conforming merchandise" drawback.

All types of drawback situations have time limits and documentary requirements which must be met in order to qualify for the refund. Goods must be exported within a certain time after importation, and the drawback claim must be made with a certain time after exportation. Before you export anything, check with your Customs Broker to see if you might be eligible for duty drawback.

Carnets

 A **carnet is a document that serves as both an entry and a bond.** It is an international customs device that allows certain types of merchandise to travel in and out of various countries without submitting the regular paperwork or paying duties. It is used mainly by people transporting sales samples and taking orders for goods.

Items entered on a carnet cannot, for the most part, be sold in the United States, and must generally be exported within a year, but there are some exceptions. A Customs Broker can set up a carnet for you, whether you are entering or leaving the United States.

Foreign Trade Zones (FTZ)

*T*his is another area that could fill an entire book - and it does, actually. It's called The U.S. Customs Foreign Trade Zones Manual. A Foreign Trade Zone is an area in the United States that is not considered "in the U.S." for certain legal purposes. There are some tax advantages in using a Zone, and merchandise can be manipulated in ways that are not possible in other types of bonded warehouses. Duty is not paid when goods are put into a Zone, but rather when they are taken out and "entered for consumption" in the United States.

One example of FTZ use to achieve a major savings in duty costs is the auto manufacturing plant. Automobile parts are dutiable are various rates, depending on what the part is. Some rates can be very high (for instance, some screws are 8.7%) and the average might be around 4-5% for all the parts used in an automobile. The duty rate for complete cars, however, is only 2.5%. An auto manufacturer can import the parts and enter them into an appropriate Foreign Trade Zone without paying the duty. The car is built in the Zone, and is then withdrawn for consumption (as a complete car) and duty is paid at the lower rate for cars.

Another use of a Foreign Trade Zone is to mark merchandise that was somehow exported from its home country without its country of origin labels. The shipment can go into a Zone in the United States for marking, and the importer does not have to deal with the pesky "marking notice" from Customs (see Chapter Eight).

 There are a few restrictions on the use of Foreign Trade Zones, however. **No item that is prohibited entry into the U.S. can be entered into a Zone** (lottery matter, immoral articles, treasonous or seditious material, and other items listed in the Customs Regulations). And no processing can be done to a textile product in a Zone, which would change the quota category. If you want to use an FTZ you must, as you are probably tired of hearing by now, find out ahead of time what rules apply to your product.

If your company decides to manufacture products in a Foreign Trade Zone, there are strict provisions for setting up and operating a Zone, from security measures to the actual handling of materials. Work with an attorney experienced in Foreign Trade Zone operations.

Bonded Warehouses

*W*arehouses that carry special Customs bonds may be used to legally defer duty payment. If your goods arrive in the U.S. during the last week in December, and the applicable duty rate is due to be reduced on January 1, it might be advantageous to warehouse the shipment for a few days. You will pay duty at the rate in effect when the goods are removed from the warehouse for consumption in the United States. Of course, there will be warehousing costs, and perhaps some additional charges by the Customs Broker, but do the arithmetic – it may be worth it.

You may also need to put merchandise in a warehouse if a quota has filled. It cannot be withdrawn until the quota opens again.

There are specific types or "classes" of warehouses, and what can be done to the goods while in the warehouse is limited by the "class."

Class 1 - These are warehouses owned or leased by the government. Most of the goods in this type of warehouse are seized, abandoned or under "general order" (G.O.) for some reason. G.O. includes unclaimed goods, or shipments for which no entry has been filed past certain time limits.

Class 2 - An importer can establish this type of warehouse for his/her own merchandise. It is exclusively for storage, however; no processing of the goods is allowed.

Class 3 - These "public bonded warehouses" are for the storage of anyone's imported goods. If you don't want to set up your own warehouse, you can, in essence, rent space in a Class 3 warehouse until you're ready for your merchandise.

Class 4 - These are bonded yards or sheds for storage of heavy or bulky items; stables, corrals and pens for livestock; and large tanks for storing bulk liquids.

Class 5 - These are for the storage of grain only.

Class 6 - Manufacturing can take place in a Class 6 warehouse, but the completed articles must be exported. One exception to the exportation rule is cigars - if the cigars are made of tobacco imported from one country, the cigars can be entered into the U.S. (I don't know - Congress writes the laws!)

Class 7 - Only smelting and refining of metals can take place in this class of warehouse, and they can be either exported or entered for consumption in the United States.

Class 8 - Under Customs supervision, this warehouse can be used for cleaning, sorting or repacking merchandise, but no manufacturing can take place.

Class 9 - These are "duty free stores." The goods are imported, put into the warehouse, and no duty is paid. They are then sold in "duty free shops" in airports and other ports of entry/exit, and they must be taken out of the United States by the purchaser. (And yes, it is illegal to buy something in a duty-free shop on your way into Mexico, drive down-river to the next port of entry, and come back into the U.S. with your duty-free purchase. Shame on you for even considering it.)

Setting up a bonded warehouse is almost as complicated as becoming a Foreign Trade Zone grantee or operator. There are stringent requirements as to construction materials, security devices and bonds, so get an expert to help you.

Articles Assembled Abroad

*I*n Chapter Six I briefly mentioned the "9802" provision in the Harmonized Tariff Schedule that allows for a partial duty elimination for goods that are assembled in a foreign country from components manufactured in the United States. The trade refers to it as the "maquiladora" or "twin plant" program because most of the early assembly plants were located along the U.S.-Mexico border, with the parent company located in the United States, supplying the components, and the assembler just across the border.

Some people still refer to it as the "807" program because that was the tariff item number in the Tariff Schedules of the United States Annotated, which pre-dated the Harmonized Tariff Schedule. The HTSUS designation is "9802.00.80." If goods fully qualify for this program, the value of the U.S.-made components is not dutiable. Essentially you pay duty only on the assembly charge and a few other items.

A few more details will give you a better idea of what's included and excluded, but this is a program that is administered on a case-by-case basis. Check with Customs ahead of time to see what documentary evidence they will require for your operations.

The "components" that are exported to be assembled must be manufactured in the United States to qualify for the duty exemption. They must be "fabricated" (no raw materials) and ready for assembly with no further processing necessary. There are some "incidental operations" that are not considered to be manufacturing operations, and will not disqualify the component.

Components which would not be eligible for the duty exemption are:

> **Foreign-made** components.
>
> **Items exported** with refunds of duty, such as drawback.
>
> **Items that were exported** to comply with law.
>
> **Goods exported** after they were processed in the U.S. under HTSUS number 9813.00.05.
>
> **Components that are further** processed by operations other than incidental operations.

The term "assembly" includes joining the components together by means of welding, riveting, gluing, sewing, soldering, force-fitting, laminating or the use of fasteners. Assembly does not include the combining of liquids, gases, chemicals, food ingredients or amorphous solids (with each other or with solid components).

Processing operations which are considered "incidental to the assembly process" do not disqualify the component from the duty exception.

These incidental operations include:

> **Trimming, filing, cutting** off small amounts of excess materials.
>
> **Cleaning, lubricating**, painting, preserving.
>
> **Small adjustments** in shape or form.
>
> **Cutting to length** or separating components for assembly.
>
> **Calibration, testing**, marking, sorting, pressing, folding.

Operations which are not considered "incidental" include significant processing, the purpose of which is fabrication, completion, or improvement of components, such as:

> **Melting substances** and pouring into a mold.
>
> **Cutting garment parts** to pattern from material.

Painting to enhance appearance.

Chemical treatment to impart new characteristics (such as permapressing, dyeing, bleaching, sanforizing, etc.).

Machining and other processes which impart new characteristics.

These are considered to be further manufacturing of the component(s) so if this type of processing occurs on a particular component, the component will be dutiable on its full value.

The value of the components is considered to be the price for which they were purchased, or their value at the time of shipment to the assembler, FOB the U.S. port of export. If the importer manufactured the components, the cost to produce them would be the value. The freight costs to ship the components to the assembler is part of the value which is dutiable.

Some of the documents you will be required to submit to Customs are:

Manufacturer(s) affidavits (to prove the components were made in the United States.

Assembler's affidavit (See Appendix G-1).

Importer's endorsement (See Appendix G-2).

List of components.

Evidence of the value of the components.

Description of the assembly operations.

Freight bills.

Export documents (from the U.S.).

Special documents and accounting records as necessary to substantiate the claim.

If yours is a related, on-going operation, you will also have to submit an annual or semi-annual "cost submission" to Customs, to update the value information you use on your entries. At the end of the accounting period (whatever you arrange with Customs) you will either get a refund of duty, or pay more, depending on whether you over- or under-estimated your value figures. NAFTA has affected the assembly program in Mexico, so "look before you leap," as they say. The assembly program is complex in terms of procedures and documents required so it's a good idea to sit down with a Customs Import Specialist in the port where your entries will be cleared to discuss the details.

What Do I Need To Do?

When you call Customs to find out the requirements for your product, ask if it is subject to Antidumping or Countervailing Duties.

Before you export anything, consult an expert to see if you would qualify for a refund of duty under the Drawback program.

If your import shipment is found to have problems, consider the use of a bonded warehouse or Foreign Trade Zone to correct the error.

Find an expert who is familiar with the spectrum of special trade programs and exemptions to help you obtain the lowest possible duty rate for your product.

References and Resources

Title 19, Code of Federal Regulations:
Part 353 (Anti-Dumping Duties)
Part 355 (Countervailing Duties)
Part 191 (Drawback)
Part 114 (Carnets)
Part 146 (Foreign Trade Zones)
Parts 19 and 144 (Warehouses)
Part 10.11 - 10.26 (Articles Assembled Abroad)

Publications are available from Boskage Commerce Publications, Ltd.
(1-888-880-4088)

Chapter Sixteen

NAFTA

Not As Free as They Anticipated

Introduction

*W*hen the North American Free Trade Agreement was discussed in the media prior to its passing into legislation, many people came away with the idea that everything would be free of duty and there would be no more paperwork for shipments traveling across the Canadian and Mexican borders of the United States. Many people also felt (and still feel) that jobs in the U.S. would disappear and companies would use cheap labor in Mexico to manufacture their products. There was also a perception that restrictions and prohibitions would be eliminated, the environment would be destroyed and U.S. businesses would suffer from the influx of duty-free goods. It was obvious that most people who talked or wrote about NAFTA had never read the Agreement, and were unaware of even its most basic provisions.

Reading the NAFTA text is a daunting project. The two volumes that comprise the rules and general provisions run about 1100 pages, and there are three additional volumes that show the duty reduction schedules for each of the three countries. **Much of the Agreement is specific to certain products or activities, though, so you would only need to read the sections that pertain to you.** If you import or export jewelry to or from Canada and/or Mexico, you can skip chapters on automotive products, textiles, investment, telecommunications, energy/oil, and agriculture, and read the rest over breakfast some morning. Well, maybe it'll take a little longer than that.

The Basics

 *N*AFTA **is an agreement signed by the United States, Mexico and Canada (hereafter referred to as the NAFTA Territory).** It has provisions for expansion, and Central and South American countries have expressed interest in joining. The Preamble of the Agreement contains a list of the goals of NAFTA. After the political rhetoric is boiled away, the objective of NAFTA is to encourage manufacturing and sourcing within the Territory, and reduce or eliminate trade barriers such as quotas and duties. The rest of the Agreement contains the rules and procedures for achieving these goals.

Many U.S. importers were disappointed to learn that not all products became duty-free as of January 1, 1994, the date NAFTA became effective. In some cases, goods that had been duty-free under the Generalized System of Preferences became dutiable, because Mexico was removed from GSP when NAFTA took effect. Total duty elimination will take place over a 15-year period, beginning January 1, 1994. Some things were free of duty immediately, others will be free at the end of five years and ten years. The last batch of dutiable merchandise will be free in the fifteenth year, 2008.

 To find out what duty rates you'll pay under NAFTA, and for how long, refer to the Annex 302.2 for the applicable country. The Annexes are separate volumes that look similar to the Harmonized Tariff Schedule, without the statistical breakouts. Look up the tariff number for your product, see what "Staging Category" it's in and what the beginning duty rate was on January 1, 1994, then refer to the Agreement to see how many years are in that category, and do the math for whatever year you're interested in. Oh, all right, I'll help you.

PVC (plastic) briefcases from Mexico, classified in 4202.12.20. The Annex 302.2 page (Appendix J-1) shows the beginning duty rate of 20% and Staging Category C. This means the product is in the ten-year phase-out group and will be duty-free as of January 1, 2003. But what duty will you pay in 1997? Since it will take ten years to become free, that means the duty is reduced by ten percent a year for ten years:

Ten percent of 20 (the duty rate) is 2. Therefore:

Beginning rate -   20%
                    - 2%
                     18% = duty in 1994
                    - 2%
                     16% = duty in 1995

Carry this calculation out until it's free of duty and you can accurately project your duty expenses:

1994 = 18%	1995 = 16%
1996 = 14%	1997 = 12%
1998 = 10%	1999 = 8%
2000 = 6%	2001 = 4%
2002 = 2%	2003 = free

The Staging Category time periods are:

A   = free as of January 1, 1994
B   = free as of January 1, 1998
B6 = free as of January 1, 1999 (textiles
        only)
C   = free as of January 1, 2003
C+ = free as of January 1, 2008
C10= free as of January 1, 2003 (textiles
        only)
D   = was already free on January 1, 1994

Rules of Origin

*I*n order to get the reduced duty rates provided by NAFTA, the product must "originate" in the NAFTA Territory. It can have material and processing input in all three countries, which is counted on the "originating" side of the equation. Any "non-originating" input (any materials or processing from any other country) counts against the qualifying content. The general rules of origin are outlined briefly below.

Rule A - Wholly Obtained or Produced. This rule says that if there is no foreign material in your product, and it was grown or manufactured in the NAFTA Territory, it qualifies as "originating." Some examples of wholly originating are flowers grown and harvested in the Territory, fish taken from territorial waters of Canada, the U.S. or Mexico, or goods produced with 100% NAFTA Territory materials. Silver jewelry made in the United States from silver mined in Mexico would qualify under Rule A, as long as there were no foreign materials used. The Agreement (and the HTSUS) contain a complete list of articles that are considered to be "wholly originating."

Pretty, simple, you say? Keep reading.

Rule B1 - Tariff Shift. This rule kicks in when the product contains some foreign material. It requires that all foreign material make a change from its own tariff number to that of the finished product, in the NAFTA Territory. Be aware that a product may be "made in" the U.S., Canada or Mexico and not be considered a NAFTA good. If you are using Criterion B tariff shift rules, the materials must make the specific tariff change shown in General Note 12, HTSUS.

To illustrate, let's use our silver jewelry example. You buy the silver, which was mined and refined in Mexico, and you make the ring and brooch settings in the United States. So far, the jewelry would qualify as originating under Rule A. However, you decide to put some semi-precious stones in the settings, which you import from China. They come to you already cut and polished and you affix them to the silver findings. These stones are non-originating (foreign) materials.

In their imported state, the Chinese stones would be classified in HTSUS number 7103.99.10. When you finish the jewelry, its tariff number is 7113.11.50. Note the change in tariff number from "loose, cut stones" to "jewelry." This is a tariff shift. But is it the correct tariff shift? We must again refer to the Harmonized Tariff Schedule, General Note

12, and find the specific tariff shift required for jewelry. The specific rule for heading 7113 (jewelry) says that the foreign materials (the stones) must undergo a tariff shift "...to headings 7113 through 7118 from any heading outside that group..." with a couple of exclusions.

Since your Chinese stones shifted from heading 7103 to 7113, and the exclusions don't apply, the finished jewelry would "originate" under Rule B1 and would be eligible for the NAFTA duty rate if you sold the jewelry to a buyer in Canada or Mexico.

 Rule B2 - Tariff Shift Plus Regional Value Content. Some specific rules in HTSUS General Note 12 require not only a tariff shift for the foreign materials, but also a Regional Value Content. A certain percentage of the appraised value (fifty or sixty percent, depending on the accounting method used by the producer) must have occurred in the NAFTA Territory.

 The Regional Value Content (RVC) is the percentage of the value of the product that represents the North American content. The main areas of the tariff schedule that require a Regional Value Content are automobiles, chemicals, footwear and machinery. There are two methods of determining RVC, and this is done by the manufacturer or producer. Since this book is for importers, the complex calculations and explanations are not covered, but if you are a producer, please refer to Part 181 of the Customs Regulations for instructions and examples. The importer of NAFTA goods will rely on a Certificate of Origin provided by the exporter, and will not be directly concerned with Regional Value Content.

 Rule B3 - Regional Value Content Only. Other specific rules of origin in HTSUS General Note 12 require only a Regional Value Content. No tariff shift need occur to qualify the good as originating. Still other specific rules give the producer a choice of meeting certain tariff shift requirements, or other, less stringent tariff shifts plus a regional value content requirement.

 Rule C - Produced in the NAFTA Territory Wholly of Originating Materials. This rule is a little harder to explain. It covers goods which are not wholly originating under Rule A, and for some reason do not meet the specific tariff shift and/or Regional Value Content rules in Rule B. Your good may still qualify if you can show that the foreign material in your product was first used to make a part or component (or processed in some other way) which was then used in the finished product. An illustration may clarify:

You are manufacturing a lamp and you buy several components from various vendors. If all the vendors can certify that the components qualify as originating materials under the NAFTA rules of origin, then your finished lamp will qualify under Rule C, made from originating materials. Under this Rule, no tariff shift or regional value content is required.

 Rule D1 - Unassembled/Disassembled Goods. This rule allows goods that are merely assembled in the NAFTA Territory to qualify as originating on the condition they meet a Regional Value Content requirement. This is difficult in most cases, since most assembly operations do not comprise fifty or sixty percent of a product's appraised value. It might cover an item which required highly skilled, intensive labor, or technical expertise for assembly, rather than just bolting or gluing parts together.

 Rule D2 - Parts Classified In the Same Heading. In some cases, parts and components would not be able to make the required tariff shift because they are classified in the same heading as the finished product. In this event, the good might still qualify as originating if the Regional Value Content requirement is met.

 Rule E - Automatic Data Processing (ADP) Goods. Rule E pertains to certain ADP goods listed in Annex 308.1 of the Agreement. These are computers, input or output units, storage units, power supplies and parts of computers in enumerated HTSUS numbers. The Rule states when all three countries in the NAFTA Territory get to the same duty rate for these products, even non-originating goods may receive the NAFTA duty rate, as long as duty has been paid once. Huh? This definitely needs an illustration.

You buy a computer from Japan and import it into Mexico

and pay duty. Then you sell the computer to a buyer in Canada. If the Mexico-Canada-U.S. NAFTA duty rates are all the same (i.e., "free") the computer would be free of duty going into Canada, even though it was made in Japan. Likewise, if the Canadian buyer then sold it to a customer in the United States, it would be duty-free when imported into the U.S.

 Rule F - Agricultural Products. This one involves certain agricultural goods, and quantitative restrictions. Get a copy of the Agreement so you can look up the various cross-references and lists of products, to see if it applies to your shipment.

Certificate of Origin

 *T*he **NAFTA Certificate of Origin is completed and signed by the exporter of the goods, and must be in the possession of the importer when the claim for NAFTA preference is made.** If, at the time the Entry Summary is filed, the importer does not have the Certificate of Origin, Column 1 duty must be paid, and a claim for refund filed when the certificate is received. The certificate does not have to be submitted with the entry paperwork, but must be produced if Customs requests it.

The Certificate of Origin may cover a single shipment, or multiple shipments for a period up to one year. **Be sure the certificate provided by the exporter describes the product completely, and all the blocks and columns are filled in.** (Note: the exporter does not have to reveal the producer's name on the Certificate of Origin, but if Customs asks the exporter for that information, it must be provided. Customs will not reveal the name to the importer, if the exporter so requests.)

If Customs finds errors or omissions in the certificate, it can be rejected and the importer might ultimately be required to pay regular duty rates for the merchandise. Also, the "country of origin" in Column 10 must be either Canada (CA), Mexico (MX) or the United States (US), or in some cases, "JNT" for a joint production. The first NAFTA certificate of origin submitted at the port of Dallas-Fort Worth in 1994 indicated "Taiwan" in Column 10. We denied the claim. The importer should keep the Certificate of Origin for five years from the date of signature.

Marking Requirements

*M*ost items still have to be marked with country of origin, even if they are NAFTA-eligible. There are a few exceptions, such as advertising samples and gifts, which do not have to be marked, but check the Regulations or ask Customs to be sure about your situation. The marking may be done in Spanish, English or French.

Post Entry Claims

*I*f goods were entered and duty paid because the importer did not have a Certificate of Origin, the claim may be made up to one year after the date of importation. This post-entry claim must establish that the goods qualified at the time of importation, even though the Certificate of Origin was not available at that time, and the certificate must be submitted with the claim. The importer must also state whether a copy of the Entry Summary was provided to anyone else, and if so, that person's name and address and the date it was provided. The claim must also state whether the importer has filed a protest of any kind on the concerned entry, or if anyone else has filed a request for refund of duties.

Verifications

*O*ccasionally, Customs will want to verify a NAFTA claim, just to keep everybody on the straight and narrow. The first thing they will do is ask the importer to provide the

Certificate of Origin. If the importer doesn't have it, the claim will be denied and the importer will be billed for the duty.

If the Certificate of Origin is provided to Customs, they may decide to verify the information on it by contacting the exporter or producer. These verifications can be done by letter, questionnaire, or an actual visit to the producer's premises. The producer must be given at least thirty days notice of Customs' intention to visit, and must grant permission. Failure of the producer to grant permission for a visit, or failure to have the pertinent records, may result in the denial of NAFTA preference for the importer's goods.

Keep in mind, the U. S. Customs Service cannot "punish" foreign manufacturers or exporters. It's the U.S. importer who will suffer if a NAFTA claim is denied. Know your suppliers and deal only with reputable companies familiar with the intricate NAFTA requirements.

That's NAFTA in a nutshell. The requirements for eligibility, marking and regional value content are very complex and require serious study if you're an exporter or producer. Importers need to have at least a passing knowledge of the Agreement's provisions so they can be assured that their records support any claims to Customs.

What Do I Need To Do?

If you import products from Mexico or Canada, be sure you have the Certificate of Origin from the exporter in your possession before claiming the NAFTA duty rate.

If you do not have the Certificate of Origin, pay the duty rate in the "General" column of the HTSUS.

If you receive a Certificate of Origin after you have paid duty, submit a request for a refund under 19 USC 1520(d) within one year from the date of importation.

If you export goods to Mexico or Canada, you must complete a Certificate of Origin for your customers. Be sure you know the Rules of Origin and have supporting documentation for all new materials and/or products.

For a more in-depth guide to qualifying products under the NAFTA rules, see *When You HAFTA Do NAFTA, Practical Solutions for the North American Free Trade Agreement*, available from Boskage Commerce Publications.

References and Resources

The North American Free Trade Agreement - all volumes available at the Government Printing Office.

Title 19, Code of Federal Regulations
Part 181 (NAFTA)
Part 102 (Rules of Origin).

Harmonized Tariff Schedule - General Note 12

NAFTA - A Guide to Customs Procedures - Customs Publication #571

Publications are available from Boskage Commerce Publications, Ltd.
(1-888-880-4088)

Chapter Seventeen

Cargo Security
A Safe Supply Chain

Introduction

*T*he Customs-Trade Partnership Against Terrorism (C-TPAT) was devised after September 11, 2001 to show that Customs was doing its share to make the country a little safer. I'm always a bit wary when the government uses the word "partnership" in naming a new program or initiative. The partnership they have in mind is one in which the importer bears all the responsibility for ensuring the integrity of cargo entering the United States. Then, if something goes wrong and your cargo is involved, your partner (Customs) will arrive to help you…to jail.

The C-TPAT program covers importers, brokers, air/ocean/rail carriers, consolidators, port authorities and terminal operators. Presumably, truck carriers will be covered by programs such as FAST (Free and Secure Trade). C-TPAT is at present a voluntary program, and signing up for it will involve a lot of internal auditing to determine where your weaknesses are. **You must develop a program to ensure security both at your facilities, and at your service/goods providers' business locations.** It will be your responsibility to train your providers and keep them updated with any changes. Processes must be developed, manuals written. Sound like a full-time job? It is, and maybe for more than one person.

If the importer does not control a facility, conveyance or process, they must make "every reasonable effort" to make the responsible party comply. Customs gets to decide whether an effort was "reasonable." They don't use the doctrine of "commercially feasible." Anything that goes wrong will be the importer's fault, because that is the only entity over which Customs has jurisdiction.

Areas to be addressed in your C-TPAT program are:

Procedures

Physical security

Access control

Personnel

Education and training

Manifests

Conveyances

Much of the desired level of security is common sense:

Have a fence with locked gates around your warehouse, and install good lighting.

Issue ID badges to employees and limit access to cargo areas.

Do background checks on employees and have a written code of conduct.

Have procedures in place to check manifests/packing lists and report overages and shortages to Customs.

The precautions regarding your providers (brokers, carriers, suppliers) may be more of a challenge:

Ensure that your provider has the financial ability to deliver goods or services contracted for.

Determine the system integrity of production processes.

Require that they do background checks, issue ID badges, limit access to cargo, etc.

Customs provides no ideas on how an importer can make a foreign company comply with all these requirements. I have seen a few questionnaires sent by U.S. importers to their overseas vendors, and some of the replies are worthy of a comedy show:

Q: Describe the lighting in and around your facility.
A: We don't need lights, we work in the daytime.

Q: Describe your process for hiring employees.
A: We get them from their previous employers.

Q: Are your employees trained to recognize illegal activity?
A: All are told to report strange phone calls or speech. Team leaders must visit their team members' family.

And my personal favorite:

Q: What actions would be taken if illegal activities were suspected or discovered:
A: NO!

You're laughing out loud, I can hear you. Customs officers would laugh, too, and then take you directly to jail if anything untoward happened with your shipment.

You should delve into C-TPAT more thoroughly by downloading the manual from the Customs website, and utilizing the handbook offered by Boskage Commerce Publications, *The Importer's Policy and Procedures Manual*, by Karin Bogue.

As with most of Customs' voluntary programs, the importer does all the work and confesses all their inadvertences discovered in self-audits. Supposedly, participation in C-TPAT provides benefits to the importer, such as:

A more secure supply chain

Fewer inspections by Customs

A Customs account manager is assigned to the importer

Access to the C-TPAT membership list

Eligibility for "account-based processes" such as monthly payments

Fewer audits by Customs

Participation does not get the importer off the hook if a violation occurs, though, even if the importer had no control over the situation.

You be the judge - do the benefits justify the expense? Talk to other importers and find out if they are happy with the program.

What Do I Need To Do?

Review the information about C-TPAT on the Customs website, www.cbp.gov

Find out if your service providers (broker, carrier, etc.) are C-TPAT certified

Engage your foreign supplier in a cargo security dialogue

References and Resources

Importer's Policy and Procedures Manual by Karin Bogue, available from Boskage Commerce Publications

Publications are available from Boskage Commerce Publications, Ltd. (1-888-880-4088)

Chapter Eighteen

Think Before You Speak

There Is Too Such a Thing as a Dumb Question

Introduction

*W*hen I left the Customs Service after twenty years (seventeen of them as an Import Specialist), my co-workers threw a party for me. I still haven't decided whether they really liked me or were just glad to see me go. At any rate, I didn't want to get maudlin and weepy, so my "goodbye speech" consisted in part of the ten dumbest questions I had ever been asked as a Customs officer. I'd like to share that list with you, and I've included the answers in case there's someone out there who has real need to know...

Q: Are we treating Shanghai the same as China for visa purposes?

A: Yes, Virginia, because Shanghai IS IN CHINA!

Q: What's the duty on goods imported from Hawaii?

A: Same as for goods imported from Oklahoma.

Q: What's the duty on knick-knacks?

A: If you've read this entire book, you know that you need a more specific description than this.

Q: Aren't baby sheep and baby goats the same thing?

A: Not to their mothers.

Q: I don't know what this stuff is - how much duty will I owe?

A: At least a million dollars. Don't import it if you don't know what it is.

Q: Is this new?

A: This question is usually asked by someone who has just been caught doing something the wrong way, and is told the correct way.

Q: How can you tell whether something is worth more than $5 a pound?

A: Ask your fourth grade arithmetic teacher to help you with the calculation.

Q: How can I tell how many is in a gross?

A: Well, when I learned this in about the third grade, it was 144, but you might want to look it up in a dictionary to make sure they haven't changed it.

Q: Do I classify the batteries in this solar calculator separately?

A: This is not really a "dumb" question. The person was somewhat technologically impaired and didn't know that solar calculators don't HAVE batteries.

Related to the Dumb Question List is the Outlandish Classification Category

T hese are totally off-the-wall tariff numbers used by people who really should have known better. I wish now I had kept a complete file of these:

I remember an entry for a date-stamping machine that was classified under the provision for "calendering machinery." At least this one had some logic to it. Never mind that the filer didn't look up the difference between "calender" and "calendar."

One of my favorites was the entry for ostrich leather using the tariff number for "furskins." I rejected the entry stating that unless those ostriches were wearing a disguise, they were classified wrong. (And my boss used to say I was sarcastic, can you imagine?)

I rejected one entry of footwear with glued-on soles, requesting that the classification number for "cement footwear" be used. The entry came back unchanged with a note reading, "They don't make shoes out of cement!" (Depends on what kind of people you hang out with.)

One cryptic description on an entry was for "hair pliers" and they were classified as a hand tool. We could only assume they were an implement used on wiry, hard-to-handle hair.

But seriously, folks, there are some questions you must ask Customs prior to importing goods and some things you shouldn't say to Customs officers.

What To Ask

Are there any restrictions on my product?

Is the country of origin of my product subject to sanctions?

Is there any antidumping or countervailing duty on my product?

Are there any other fees besides duty?

Are there any copyright, trademark or patent issues involved?

Are there any special marking requirements?

Do any other agencies regulate my product?

What is the duty rate?

Do I need any special forms, declarations or certifications?

What is the "informal" entry limit?

Consider making an appointment to see an Import Specialist at Customs (or have them come to your premises and talk to you) and discuss your product and your import operation. Provide a sample. Discuss value.

Oh, and by the way - if you call the Customs office, have a piece of paper and pencil ready to take notes. You will get more information than you can possibly remember.

Things Customs Might Ask You

What is your product?

What is it made of?

What is its principal use in the United States?

How is it sold?

How will it be packaged?

Are you the end-user, or will you re-sell it?

Where was it made?

Did you provide any materials or tools to the manufacturer?

Depending on the product, the questions can be general in nature (What is it made of? Wood.) or very technical (Is this high speed tool steel, containing molybdenum, tungsten, vanadium or chromium? How much of each?). Sometimes you'll need to know the scientific name of the animal whose skin decorates your product, or the ingredients in foodstuffs. If you are importing electronics, you may need to know the country where the printed circuit boards were loaded. **In order to give you correct information, Customs must get correct information from you.** You may need to talk to them more than once prior to importing your goods.

Things NOT To Say

*T*here are a few things you should NEVER say to Customs. Here's a sample:

We [always][never] did it this way before.
If you say this, Customs will look up your old entries and send you a REALLY big bill, or start an investigation.

[New York][Los Angeles] doesn't make us do it this way.
As hard as they try, Customs procedures are not always uniform from port to port. Maybe they just aren't looking at your shipments in NY or LA. Don't bring it up unless you want Customs to notify NY and LA that there's a problem with your entries.

Is this new?
See list of Dumb Questions.

I didn't know that $30,000 diamond necklace was in my luggage, because my wife packed my suitcase.
Yeah, right.

I bet you Customs people [eat][drink][smoke] it when you take it away from me.
They really don't. They'd rather watch you watch them pour your expensive booze down the sink.

Hurry up and clear this flight - I've been cooped up on that plane for eight hours, and I'm tired.
Well, being cooped up on that airplane, eating, drinking and sleeping whenever you want, maybe watching a movie, is a lot better than examining cargo all day, then having to wait on your LATE flight, and then spending two more hours listening to people WHINE...

I thought everything is free from Mexico because of NAFTA.
See Chapter 16.

I want to file my own entries.
No you don't, you really don't...

And the absolute worst thing you can say to any government employee:

I'm a taxpayer and I pay your salary.
They pay taxes, too. So that means they pay their own salaries, right? Whenever anyone used this line on me, I stopped helping them and immediately reverted to the letter of the law. You cannot intimidate a federal law enforcement officer, so don't even try. They are not impressed by the fact that you know a Senator or the President of the United States or the King of Siam, or the richest man in the state. If you are truly having a major problem with an officer, ask to speak to the person's supervisor. Remember, you haven't cleared Customs until Customs says you've cleared Customs!

Appendix A-1

THE CUSTOMS MODERNIZATION ACT

Section Titles

Section 611 -	Penalties for Violations of Arrival, Reporting, Entry and Clearance Requirements
Section 612 -	Failure to Declare
Section 613 -	Customs Testing Laboratories; Detention of Merchandise
Section 614 -	Recordkeeping
Section 615 -	Examination of Books and Witnesses
Section 616 -	Judicial Enforcement
Section 617 -	Review of Protests
Section 618 -	Repeal of Provision Relating to Reliquidation on Account of Fraud
Section 619 -	Penalties Relating to Manifests
Section 620 -	Unlawful Unlading or Transshipment
Section 621 -	Penalties for Fraud, Gross Negligence and Negligence; Prior Disclosure
Section 622 -	Penalties for False Drawback Claims
Section 623 -	Interpretive Rulings and Decisions; Public Information
Section 624 -	Seizure Authority
(Section 625 to 630 not used)	
Section 631 -	National Customs Automation Program

Appendix A-2

REASONABLE CARE CHECKLIST

AGENCY: U. S. Customs Service, Department of the Treasury

ACTION: General notice.

SUMMARY: This document sets forth, for guidance, a checklist of measures which importers and their agents may find helpful in meeting the "reasonable care" requirements of the Customs laws.

DATE: Effective upon publication.

FOR FURTHER INFORMATION CONTACT: Robert Pisani, Penalties Branch, International Trade Compliance Division, Office of Regulations and Rulings, (202) 927-1203.

Preamble: One of the most significant effects of the Customs Modernization Act is the establishment of the clear requirement that parties exercise "reasonable care" in importing into the United States. Section 484 of the Tariff Act, as amended, requires an importer of record using reasonable care "to make entry by filing such information as is necessary to enable the Customs Service to determine whether the merchandise may be released from customs custody," and using reasonable care-"complete the entry by filing with the Customs Service the declared value, classification and rate of duty" and "such other documentation ... or information as is necessary to enable the Customs Service to ... properly assess duties ... collect accurate statistics ... determine whether any other applicable requirement of law ... is met." Despite the seemingly simple connotation of the term "reasonable care," this explicit responsibility defies easy explanation. The facts and circumstances surrounding every import transaction differ-from the experience of the importer to the nature of the imported articles. Consequently, neither the Customs Service nor the importing community can develop a foolproof reasonable care "checklist" which would cover every import transaction. On the other hand, In keeping with the Modernization Act's theme of "informed compliance," the Customs Service would like to take this opportunity to recommend that the importing community examine the list of questions below. In Customs view, the list of questions may prompt or suggest a program, framework or methodology which importers may find useful in avoiding compliance problems and meeting "reasonable care" responsibilities.

Obviously, the questions below cannot be exhaustive or encyclopedic; ordinarily, every import transaction is different. For the same reason, it cannot be overemphasized that although the following information is provided to promote enhanced compliance with the Customs laws and regulations, it has no legal, binding or precedential effect on Customs or the importing community. In this regard, Customs notes that the checklist is not an attempt to create a presumption of negligence, but rather, an attempt to educate, inform and provide guidance to the importing community. Consequently, Customs believes that the following information may be helpful to the importing community and hopes that this document will facilitate and encourage importers to develop their own unique compliance measurement plans, reliable procedures and "reasonable care" programs.

As a convenience to the public, the checklist also includes the text of a checklist previously published in the Federal Register for use in certain textile and apparel importations. The full document was published in 62 FR 48340 (September 15, 1997).

As a final reminder, it should be noted that to further assist the importing community, Customs issues rulings and informed compliance publications on a variety of technical subjects and processes. It is strongly recommended that importers always make sure that they are using the latest versions of these publications.

General Questions For All Transactions

Asking and answering the following questions will assist importers in the exercise of Reasonable Care

1. If you have not retained an expert to assist you in complying with Customs requirements, do you have access to the Customs Regulations (Title 19 of the Code of Federal Regulations), the Harmonized Tariff Schedule of the United States, and the GPO publication "Customs Bulletin and Decisions?" Do you have access to the Customs Internet Website, Customs Electronic Bulletin Board or other research service to permit you to establish reliable procedures and facilitate compliance with Customs laws and regulations?

2. Has a responsible and knowledgeable individual within your organization reviewed the Customs documentation prepared by you or your expert to ensure that it is full, complete and accurate? If that documentation was prepared outside your own organization, do you have a reliable system in place to insure that you receive copies of the information as submitted to Customs; that it is reviewed for accuracy; and that Customs is timely apprised of any needed corrections?

3. If you use an expert to assist you in complying with Customs requirements, have you discussed your importations in advance with that person and have you provided that person with full, complete and accurate information about the import transactions?

4. Are identical transactions or merchandise handled differently at different ports or Customs offices within the same port? If so, have you brought this to the attention of the appropriate Customs officials?

Merchandise Description & Tariff Classification

Basic Question: Do you know or have you established a reliable procedure or program to ensure that you know what you ordered, where it was made and what it is made of?

1. Have you provided or established reliable procedures to ensure you provide a complete and accurate description of your merchandise to Customs in accordance with 19 U.S.C. 1481? (Also, see 19 CFR 141.87 and 19 CFR 141.89 for special merchandise description requirements.)

2. Have you provided or established reliable procedures to ensure you provide a correct tariff classification of your merchandise to Customs in accordance with 19 U.S.C. 1484?

3. Have you obtained a Customs "ruling" regarding the description of the merchandise or its tariff classification (See 19 CFR Part 177), and if so, have you established reliable procedures to ensure that you have followed the ruling and brought it to Customs attention?

4. Where merchandise description or tariff classification information is not immediately available, have you established a reliable procedure for providing that information, and is the procedure being followed?

5. Have you participated in a Customs pre-classification of your merchandise relating to proper merchandise description and classification?

6. Have you consulted the tariff schedules, Customs informed compliance publications, court cases and/or Customs rulings to assist you in describing and classifying the merchandise?

7. Have you consulted with a Customs "expert" (e.g., lawyer, Customs Broker, accountant, or Customs consultant) to assist in the description and/or classification of the merchandise?

8. If you are claiming a conditionally free or special tariff classification/provision for your merchandise (e.g., GSP, HTSUS Item 9802, NAFTA, etc.), How have you verified that the merchandise qualifies for such status? Have you obtained or developed reliable procedures to obtain any required or necessary documentation to support the claim? If making a NAFTA preference claim, do you already have a NAFTA certificate of origin in your possession?

9. Is the nature of your merchandise such that a laboratory analysis or other specialized procedure is suggested to assist in proper description and classification?

10. Have you developed a reliable program or procedure to maintain and produce any required Customs entry documentation and supporting information?

Valuation

Basic Questions: Do you know or have you established reliable procedures to know the "price actually paid or payable" for your merchandise? Do you know the terms of sale; whether there will be rebates, tie-ins, indirect costs, additional payments; whether "assists" were provided, commissions or royalties paid? Are amounts actual or estimated? Are you and the supplier "related parties?"

1. Have you provided or established reliable procedures to provide Customs with a proper declared value for your merchandise in accordance with 19 U.S.C. 1484 and 19 U.S.C. 140la?

2. Have you obtained a Customs "ruling" regarding the valuation of the merchandise (See 19 CFR Part 177), and if so, have you established reliable procedures to ensure that you have followed the ruling and brought it to Customs attention?

3. Have you consulted the Customs valuation laws and regulations, Customs Valuation Encyclopedia, Customs informed compliance publications, court cases and Customs rulings to assist you in valuing merchandise?

4. Have you consulted with a Customs "expert" (e.g., lawyer, accountant, Customs Broker, Customs consultant) to assist in the valuation of the merchandise?

5. If you purchased the merchandise from a "related" seller, have you established procedures to ensure that you have reported that fact upon entry and taken measures or established reliable procedures to ensure that value reported to Customs meets one of the "related party" tests?

6. Have you taken measures or established reliable procedures to ensure that all of the legally required costs or payments associated with the imported merchandise have been reported to Customs (e.g., assists, all commissions, indirect payments or rebates, royalties, etc.)?

7. If you are declaring a value based on a transaction in which you were/are not the buyer, have you substantiated that the transaction is a bona fide sale at arm's length and that the merchandise was clearly destined to the United States at the time of sale?

8. If you are claiming a conditionally free or special tariff classification/provision for your merchandise (e.g., GSP, HTSUS Item 9802, NAFTA, etc.), have you established a reliable system or program to ensure that you reported the required value information and obtained any required or necessary documentation to support the claim?

9. Have you established a reliable program or procedure to produce any required entry documentation and supporting information?

Country of Origin/Marking/Quota

Basic Question: Have you taken reliable measures to ascertain the correct country of origin for the imported merchandise?

1. Have you established reliable procedures to ensure that you report the correct country of origin on Customs entry documents?

2. Have you established reliable procedures to verify or ensure that the merchandise is properly marked upon entry with the correct country of origin (if required) in accordance with 19 U.S.C. 1304 and any other applicable special marking requirement (watches, gold, textile labeling, etc)?

3. Have you obtained a Customs "ruling" regarding the proper marking and country of origin of the merchandise (See 19 CFR Part 177), and if so, have you established reliable procedures to ensure that you followed the ruling and brought it to Customs attention?

4. Have you consulted with a Customs "expert" (e.g., lawyer, accountant, Customs Broker, Customs consultant) regarding the correct country of origin/proper marking of your merchandise?

5. Have you taken reliable and adequate measures to communicate Customs country of origin marking requirements to your foreign supplier prior to importation of your merchandise?

6. If you are claiming a change in the origin of the merchandise or claiming that the goods are of U.S. origin, have you taken required measures to substantiate your claim (e.g. Do

you have U.S. milling certificates or manufacturer's affidavits attesting to the production in the U.S.)?

7. If you are importing textiles or apparel, have you developed reliable procedures to ensure that you have ascertained the correct country of origin in accordance with 19 U.S.C. 3592 (Section 334, Pub. Law 103-465) and assured yourself that no illegal transshipment or false or fraudulent practices were involved?

8. Do you know how your goods are made from raw materials to finished goods, by whom and where?

9. Have you checked with Customs and developed a reliable procedure or system to ensure that the quota category is correct?

10. Have you checked or developed reliable procedures to check the Status Report on Current Import Quotas (Restraint Levels) issued by Customs to determine if your goods are subject to a quota category which has "part" categories?

11. Have you taken reliable measures to ensure that you have obtained the correct visas for your goods if they are subject to visa categories?

12. In the case of textile articles, have you prepared or developed a reliable program to prepare the proper country declaration for each entry, i.e., a single country declaration (if wholly obtained/produced) or a multi-country declaration (if raw materials from one country were produced into goods in a second)?

13. Have you established a reliable maintenance program or procedure to ensure you can produce any required entry documentation and supporting information, including any required certificates of origin?

Intellectual Property Rights

Basic Question: Have you determined or established a reliable procedure to permit you to determine whether your merchandise or its packaging bear or use any trademarks or copyrighted matter or are patented and, if so, that you have a legal right to import those items into, and/or use those items in, the U.S.?

1. If you are importing goods or packaging bearing a trademark registered in the U.S., have you checked or established a reliable procedure to ensure that it is genuine and not restricted from importation under the "gray-market" or parallel import requirements of U.S. law (see 19 CFR 133.2 1), or that you have permission from the trademark holder to import such merchandise?

2. If you are importing goods or packaging which consist of, or contain registered copyrighted material, have you checked or established a reliable procedure to ensure that it is authorized and genuine? If you are importing sound recordings of live performances, were the recordings authorized?

3. Have you checked or developed a reliable procedure to see if your merchandise is subject to an International Trade Commission or court ordered exclusion order?

4. Have you established a reliable procedure to ensure that you maintain and can produce any required entry documentation and supporting information?

Miscellaneous Questions

1. Have you taken measures or developed reliable procedures to ensure that your merchandise complies with other agency requirements (e.g., FDA, EPA/DOT, CPSC, FTC, Agriculture, etc.) prior to or upon entry, including the procurement of any necessary licenses or permits?

2. Have you taken measures or developed reliable procedures to check to see if your goods are subject to a Commerce Department dumping or countervailing duty investigation or determination, and if so, have you complied or developed reliable procedures to ensure compliance with Customs reporting requirements upon entry (e.g., 19 CFR 141.61)?

3. Is your merchandise subject to quota/visa requirements, and if so, have you provided or developed a reliable procedure to provide a correct visa for the goods upon entry?

4. Have you taken reliable measures to ensure and verify that you are filing the correct type of Customs entry (e.g., TIB, T&E, consumption entry, mail entry, etc.), as well as ensure that you have the right to make entry under the Customs Regulations?

Additional Questions for Textile and Apparel Importers

Note: Section 333 of the Uruguay Round Implementation Act (19 U.S.C. 1592a) authorizes the Secretary of the Treasury to publish a list of foreign producers, manufacturers, suppliers, sellers, exporters, or other foreign persons who have been found to have violated 19 U.S.C. 1592 by using certain false, fraudulent or counterfeit documentation, labeling, or prohibited transshipment practices in connection with textiles and apparel products.

Section 1592a also requires any importer of record entering, introducing, or attempting to introduce into the commerce of the United States textile or apparel products that were either directly or indirectly produced, manufactured, supplied, sold, exported, or transported by such named person to show, to the satisfaction of the Secretary, that such importer has exercised reasonable care to ensure that the textile or apparel products are accompanied by documentation, packaging, and labeling that are accurate as to its origin.

Under section 1592a, reliance solely upon information regarding the imported product from a person named on the list does not constitute the exercise of reasonable care. Textile and apparel importers who have some commercial relationship with one or more of the listed parties must exercise a degree of reasonable care in ensuring that the documentation covering the imported merchandise, as well as its packaging and labeling, is accurate as to the country of origin of the merchandise. This degree of reasonable care must rely on more than information supplied by the named party.

In meeting the reasonable care standard when importing textile or apparel products and when dealing with a party named on the list published pursuant to section 592A an importer should consider the following questions in attempting to ensure that the documentation, packaging, and labeling is accurate as to the country of origin of the imported merchandise. The list of questions is not exhaustive but is illustrative.

1. Has the importer had a prior relationship with the named party?

2. Has the importer had any detentions and/or seizures of textile or apparel products that were directly or indirectly produced, supplied, or transported by the named party?

3. Has the importer visited the company's premises and ascertained that the company has the capacity to produce the merchandise?

4. Where a claim of an origin conferring process is made in accordance with 19 CFR 102.2 1, has the importer ascertained that the named party actually performed the required process?

5. Is the named party operating from the same country as is represented by that party on the documentation, packaging or labeling?

6. Have quotas for the imported merchandise closed or are they nearing closing from the main producer countries for this commodity?

7. What is the history of this country regarding this commodity?

8. Have you asked questions of your supplier regarding the origin of the product?

9. Where the importation is accompanied by a visa, permit, or license, has the importer verified with the supplier or manufacturer that the visa, permit, and/or license is both valid and accurate as to its origin? Has the importer scrutinized the visa, permit or license as to any regularities that would call its authenticity into question?

Dated: December 1, 1997.

Appendix A-3

(a)(1)(A) LIST
List of Records Required for the Entry of Merchandise

... Section 509(a)(1)(A) of the Tariff Act of 1930, as amended by title VI of Public Law 103-182, commonly referred to as the Customs Modernization Act (19 U.S.C. 1509(a)(1)(A)), requires the production, within a reasonable time after demand by CBP is made (taking into consideration the number, type and age of the item demanded) if "such record is required by law or regulation for the entry of the merchandise (whether or not CBP required its presentation at the time of entry)." Section 509(e) of the Tariff Act of 1930, as amended by Public Law 103-182 (19 U.S.C. 1509(e)) requires CBP to identify and publish a list of the records and entry information that is required to be maintained and produced under subsection (a)(1)(A) of section 509...These may change...

...Not every entry of merchandise requires all of the following information ... When a record or information is filed with and retained by CBP, the record is not subject to record keeping penalties, although the underlying backup or supporting information from which it is obtained may also be subject to the general record retention regulations, and examination or summons pursuant to 19 U.S.C. 1508 and 1509...

(The above paragraphs were edited for reproduction in this book. Many other records are required to be kept and provided to Customs, but the documents listed on the (a)(1)(A) List are the only ones against which Customs can issue a penalty for failure to maintain or produce. Consult the full text of this provision of P. L. 108-132.)

LIST OF RECORDS AND INFORMATION REQUIRED FOR THE ENTRY OF MERCHANDISE

The following records (which includes, but is not limited to, any statement, declaration, document, or electronically generated or machine readable data) are required by law or regulation for the entry of merchandise and are required to be maintained and produced to Customs upon reasonable demand (whether or not Customs required its presentation at the time of entry). Information may be submitted to Customs at time of entry in a Customs authorized electronic or paper format. Not every entry of merchandise requires all of the following information. Only those records or information applicable to the entry requirements for the merchandise in question will be required/mandatory. The list may be amended as Customs reviews its requirements and continues to implement the Customs Modernization Act. When a record or information is filed with and retained by Customs, the record is not subject to record keeping penalties, although the underlying backup or supporting information from which it is obtained may also be subject to the general record retention regulations and examination or summons pursuant to 19 U.S.C. 1508 and 1509.

(All references, unless otherwise indicated, are to title 19, Code of Federal Regulations, April 1, 1995 Edition, as amended by subsequent Federal Register notices.)

I. General list or records required for most entries. Information shown with an asterisk (*) is usually on the appropriate form and filed with and retained by Customs:

SECTION

141.11-.15	Evidence of right to make entry (airway bill/bill of lading or *carrier certificate, etc.) when goods are imported on a common carrier.
141.19	*Declaration of entry (usually contained on the Entry Summary or warehouse entry)

141.32	Power of attorney (when required by regulations)
141.54	Consolidated shipments authority to make entry (if this procedure is utilized)
142.3	Packing list (where appropriate)
142.4	Bond information (except if 10.101 or 142.4(c) applies)
Parts 4,18, 122,123	*Vessel, Vehicle or Air Manifest (filed by the carrier)

II. The following records or information are required by 141.61 on Customs Form (CF) 3461 or CF 7533 or the regulations cited.

Information shown with an asterisk (*) is contained on the appropriate form and/or otherwise filed with and retained by Customs:

142.3, .3a	*Entry Number *Entry Type Code *Elected Entry Date *Port Code
142.4	*Bond information
141.61,142.3a	*Broker/Importer Filer Number
141.61,142.3	*Ultimate Consignee Name and Number /street address of premises to be delivered
141.61	*Importer of Record Number *Country of Origin
141.11	*IT/BL/AWB Number and Code *Arrival Date
141.61	*Carrier Code *Voyage/Flight/Trip *Vessel Code/Name *Manufacturer ID Number (for AD/CVD must be actual mfr.) *Location of Goods-Code(s)/Name(s) *U.S. Port of Unlading

	*General Order Number (only when required by the regulations)
142.6	*Description of Merchandise
142.6	*HTSUS Number
142.6	*Manifest Quantity *Total Value *Signature of Applicant

III. In addition to the information listed above, the following records or items of information are required by law and regulation for the entry of merchandise and are presently required to be produced by the importer of record at the time the Customs Form 7501 is filed.

141.61	*Entry Summary Date
141.61	*Entry Date
142.3	*Bond Number, Bond Type Code and Surety code
142.3	*Ultimate Consignee Address
141.61	*Importer of Record Name and Address
141.61	*Exporting Country and Date Exported *I.T. (In-bond) Entry Date (for IT Entries only) *Mode of Transportation (MOT Code)
141.61	*Importing Carrier Name
141.82	Conveyance Name/Number *Foreign Port of Lading *Import Date and Line Numbers *Reference Number *HTSUS Number
141.61	*Identification number for merchandise subject to Anti-dumping or Countervailing duty order (ADA/CVD Case Number)
141.61	*Gross Weight *Manifest Quantity
141.61	*Net Quantity in HTSUS Units

141.61	*Entered Value, Charges, and Relationship
141.61	*Applicable HTSUS Rate, ADA/CVD Rate, I.R.C. Rate, and/or Visa Number, Duty, I.R. Tax, and Fees (e.g. HMF, MPF, Cotton)
141.61	Non-Dutiable Charges
141.61	*Signature of Declarant, Title, and Date *Textile Category Number
141.83,.86	Invoice information which includes-e.g., date, number, merchandise (commercial product) description, quantities, values, unit price, trade terms, part, model, style, marks and numbers, name and address of foreign party responsible for invoicing, kind of currency Terms of Sale Shipping Quantities Shipping Units of Measurements Manifest Description of Goods Foreign Trade Zone Designation and Status Designation (if applicable) Indication of Eligibility for Special Access Program (9802/GSP/CBI)
141.89	CF 5523
141.89, et al	Corrected Commercial Invoice
141.86 (e)	Packing List
177.8	*Binding Ruling Identification Number (or a copy of the ruling)
10.102	Duty Free Entry Certificate (9808.00.30009 HTSUS)
10.108	Lease Statement

IV. Documents/records or information required for entry of special categories of merchandise (The listed documents or information is only required for merchandise entered (or required to be entered) in accordance with the provisions of the sections of 19 CFR (the Customs Regulations) listed). These are In addition to any documents/records or information required by other agencies in their regulations for the entry of merchandise:

4.14	CF 226 Information for vessel repairs, parts and equipment
7.3(f)	CF 3229 Origin certificate for insular possessions, Shipper's and Importer's declarations for insular possessioons
Part 10	Documents required for entry of articles exported and returned:
10.1-10.6	Foreign shipper's declaration or master's certificate, declaration for free entry by owner, importer or consignee
10.7	Certificate from foreign shipper for reusable containers
10.8	Declaration of person performing alterations or repairs Declaration for non-conforming merchandise
10.9	Declaration of processing
10.24	Declaration by assembler endorsement by importer
10.31,.35	Documents required for Temporary Importations Under Bond: Information required, Bond or Carnet
10.36	Lists for samples, professional equipment, theatrical effects Documents required for Instruments of International Traffic:
10.41	Application, Bond or TIR carnet Note: additional 19 U.S.C. 1508 records: see 10.41b(e)
10.43	Documents required for exempt organizations
10.46	Request from head of agency for 9808.00.10 or 9808.00.20 HTSUS treatment Documents required for works of art

10.48	Declaration of artist, seller or shipper, curator, etc
10.49,.52	Declaration by institution
10.53	Declaration by importer USFWS Form 3-177, if appropriate
10.59,.63	Documents/ CF 5125/ for withdrawal of ship supplies
10.66,.67	Declarations for articles exported and returned
10.68.,69	Documents for commercial samples, tools, theatrical effects
10.70,.71	Purebred breeding certificate
10.84	Automotive Products certificate
10.90	Master records and metal matrices: detailed statement of cost of production.
10.98	Declarations for copper fluxing material
10.99	Declaration of non-beverage ethyl alcohol, ATF permit
10.101-.102	Stipulation for government shipments and/or certification for government duty-free entries, etc.
10.107	Report for rescue and relief equipment
15 CFR 301	Requirements for entry of scientific and educational apparatus
10.121	Certificate from USIA for visual/auditory materials
10.134	Declaration of actual use (When classification involves actual use)
10.138	End Use Certificate
10.171	Documents, etc. required for entries of GSP merchandise
10.173,10.175	GSP Declaration (plus supporting documentation)
10.174	Evidence of direct shipment

10.179	Certificate of importer of crude petroleum
10.180	Certificate of fresh, chilled or frozen beef
10.183	Civil aircraft parts/simulator documentation and certifications
10.191-.198	Documents, etc. required for entries of CBI merchandise CBI declaration of origin (plus supporting information)
10.194	Evidence of direct shipment
10.199	Documents, etc., required for duty-free entry of spirituous beverages
	produced in Canada from CBI rum, declaration of Canadian
	processor, plus supporting information
10.216	AGOA Textile certificate of origin and supporting records
10.226	CBTPA Textile certificate of origin and supporting records
10.228	CBTPA Declaration of Compliance for brassieres
10.236	CBTPA Non-textile certificate of origin and supporting records
10.246	ATPDEA Textile certificate of origin
10.248	ATPDEA Declaration of Compliance for brassieres
10.256	ATPDEA Non-textile certificate of origin
[10.306	Evidence of direct shipment for CFTA]
[10.307	Documents, etc. required for entries under CFTA Certificate of origin of CF 353]

[CFTA provisions are suspended while NAFTA remains in effect. See part 181]

| 12.6 | European Community cheese affidavit |

12.7	HHS permit for milk or cream importation
12.11	Notice of arrival for plant and plant products
12.17	APHIS Permit animal viruses, serums and toxins
12.21	HHS license for viruses, toxins, antitoxins, etc for treatment of man
12.23	Notice of claimed investigational exemption for a new drug
12.26-.31	Necessary permits from APHIS, FWS & foreign government certificates when required by the applicable regulation
12.33	Chop list, proforma invoice and release permit from HHS
12.34	Certificate of match inspection and importer's declaration
12.43	Certificate of origin/declarations for goods made by forced labor, etc.
12.61	Shipper's declaration, official certificate for seal and otter skins
12.73 12.80	Motor vehicle declarations
12.85	Boat declarations(CG-5096) and USCG exemption
12.91	FDA form 2877 and required declarations for electronics products
12.99	Declarations for switchblade knives
12.104-.104I	Cultural property declarations, statements and certificates of origin
12.105-.109	Pre-Columbian monumental and architectural sculpture and murals certificate of legal exportation evidence of exemption
12.110	Pesticides, etc. notice of arrival
12.118-.127	Toxic substances: TSCA statements

12.130	Textiles & textile products Single country declaration Multiple country declaration VISA
12.132	NAFTA textile requirements
12.140	Province of first manufacture, export permit number and fee status of softwood lumber from Canada
54.5	Declaration by importer of use of use of certain metal articles
54.6 (a)	Re-Melting Certificate
113 App B	Bond to indemnify complainant under Sec 337 TA 1930 as amended
114	Carnets (serves as entry and bond document where applicable)
115	Container certificate of approval
128	Express consignments
128.21	*Manifests with required information (filed by carrier)
132.15, 132.17	Export certificates for beef or sugar-containing products subject to tariff rate quotas
132.18	License or written authorization for worsted wool fabric subject to tariff rate quota
132.23	Acknowledgment of delivery for mailed items subject to quota
133.21(b)(6)	Consent from trademark or trade name holder to import otherwise restricted goods
134.25,.36	Certificate of marking; notice to repacker
141.88	Computed value information
141.89	Additional invoice information required for certain classes of merchandise including, but not limited to:

Textile Entries: Quota charge Statement, if applicable including Style Number, Article Number and Product

Steel Entries: Ordering specifications, including but not limited to, all applicable industry standards and mill certificates, including but not limited to, chemical composition.

143.13	Documents required for appraisement entries bills, statements of costs of production value declaration
143.23	Informal entry: commercial invoice plus declaration
144.12	Warehouse entry information
145.11	Customs Declaration for Mail, Invoice
145.12	Mail entry information (CF 3419 is completed by Customs but formal entry may be required.)
148	Supporting documents for personal importations
151 subpart B	Scale Weight
151 subpart B	Sugar imports sampling/lab information (Chemical Analysis)
151 subpart C	Petroleum imports sampling/lab information Out turn Report 24. to 25. - Reserved
151 subpart E	Wool and Hair invoice information, additional documents
151 subpart F	Cotton invoice information, additional documents
181.22	NAFTA Certificate of origin and supporting record
19 USC 1356k	Coffee Form O (currently suspended)

Other Federal and State Agency Documents

State and Local Government Records

Other Federal Agency Records (See 19 CFR Part 12, 19 U.S.C. 1484, 1499)

Licenses, Authorizations, Permits

Foreign Trade Zones

146.32   Supporting documents to CF 214

Appendix B

INVOICE

Good Factory Company, Ltd.
10th Fl. No. 883, Lane 6, Sui-Due
Tan Sue, Taipei, Taiwan, R.O.C.
(Tel: (86) 878-1111 Fax: (86) 801-8899

For Account of: Importer's Imports, Inc.   No.: 12345
                         1000 Madein Lane   Date: March 1,2002
                         Dallas, Texas 75222
                         U.S.A.

Shipment from: Taipei, Taiwan to Dallas, TX
Shipment via: Air
Country of Origin: Taiwan

Item No.	Description	P.O.#	Quantity	Unit Price	Total Price
X14922	Widget, steel	175	75M	5.00/m	US $375.00
X3345N	Do-Dad, plastic	175	250 ea	2.99/ea	747.50
T9989D	Frammis	175	100 ea	11.00/ea	1100.00
			75M and 350/ea	FOB	US $2222.50

Say U.S. dollars Two Thousand Two Hundred Twenty-two and fifty
cents only.

Shipping marks:
Importers Imports
U.S.A.

repair parts

Dallas, Texas
MADE IN TAIWAN
c/no. 1-15

                         _____
                         Good Factory Company, Ltd.

Appendix C

General Rules of Interpretation

Harmonized Tariff Schedule of the United States (2005)

GENERAL RULES OF INTERPRETATION

Classification of goods in the tariff schedule shall be governed by the following principles:

1. The table of contents, alphabetical index, and titles of sections, chapters and subchapters are provided for ease of reference only; for legal purposes, classification shall be determined according to the terms of the headings and any relative section or chapter notes and, provided such headings or notes do not otherwise require, according to the following provisions:

2. (a) Any reference in a heading to an article shall be taken to include a reference to that article incomplete or unfinished, provided that, as entered, the incomplete or unfinished article has the essential character of the complete or finished article. It shall also include a reference to that article complete or finished (or falling to be classified as complete or finished by virtue of this rule), entered unassembled or disassembled.

   (b) Any reference in a heading to a material or substance shall be taken to include a reference to mixtures or combinations of that material or substance with other materials or substances. Any reference to goods of a given material or substance shall be taken to include a reference to goods consisting wholly or partly of such material or substance. The classification of goods consisting of more than one material or substance shall be according to the principles of rule 3.

3. When, by application of rule 2(b) or for any other reason, goods are, prima facie, classifiable under two or more headings, classification shall be effected as follows:

(a) The heading which provides the most specific description shall be preferred to headings providing a more general description. However, when two or more headings each refer to part only of the materials or substances contained in mixed or composite goods or to part only of the items in a set put up for retail sale, those headings are to be regarded as equally specific in relation to those goods, even if one of them gives a more complete or precise description of the goods.

(b) Mixtures, composite goods consisting of different materials or made up of different components, and goods put up in sets for retail sale, which cannot be classified by reference to 3(a), shall be classified as if they consisted of the material or component which gives them their essential character, insofar as this criterion is applicable.

(c) When goods cannot be classified by reference to 3(a) or 3(b), they shall be classified under the heading which occurs last in numerical order among those which equally merit consideration.

4. Goods which cannot be classified in accordance with the above rules shall be classified under the heading appropriate to the goods to which they are most akin.

5. In addition to the foregoing provisions, the following rules shall apply in respect of the goods referred to therein:

(a) Camera cases, musical instrument cases, gun cases, drawing instrument cases, necklace cases and similar containers, specially shaped or fitted to contain a specific article or set of articles, suitable for longterm use and entered with the articles for which they are intended, shall be classified with such articles when of a kind normally sold therewith. This rule does not, however, apply to containers which give the whole its essential character;

(b) Subject to the provisions of rule 5(a) above, packing materials and packing containers entered with the goods therein shall be classified with the goods if they are of a kind normally used for packing such goods. However, this provision is not binding when such packing materials or packing containers are clearly suitable for repetitive use.

6. For legal purposes, the classification of goods in the subheadings of a heading shall be determined according to the terms of those subheadings and any related subheading notes and, mutatis mutandis, to the above rules, on the understanding that only subheadings at the same level are comparable. For the purposes of this rule, the relative section, chapter and subchapter notes also apply, unless the context otherwise requires.

ADDITIONAL U.S. RULES OF INTERPRETATION

1. In the absence of special language or context which otherwise requires

(a) a tariff classification controlled by use (other than actual use) is to be determined in accordance with the use in the United States at, or immediately prior to, the date of importation, of goods of that class or kind to which the imported goods belong, and the controlling use is the principal use;

(b) a tariff classification controlled by the actual use to which the imported goods are put in the United States is satisfied only if such use is intended at the time of importation, the goods are so used and proof thereof is furnished within 3 years after the date the goods are entered;

(c) a provision for parts of an article covers products solely or principally used as a part of such articles but a provision for "parts" or "parts and accessories" shall not prevail over a specific provision for such part or accessory; and

(d) the principles of section XI regarding mixtures of two or more textile materials shall apply to the classification of goods in any provision in which a textile material is named.

Appendix D

RELATED PARTIES

UNDER NAFTA

1. Officers/directors of one another's business

2. Legally recognized partners

3. Employer and employee

4. Owns/controls 25% or more voting stock/shares of the other

5. One controls the other directly or indirectly

6. Both are controlled by a third party

7. Members of the same family (natural or adopted children, brothers, sisters, parents, grandparents or spouses)

NON-NAFTA

1. Officers/directors of one another's business

2. Legally recognized partners

3. Employer and employee

4. Owns/controls 5% or more voting stock/shares of the other

5. Parties owning / controlling or controlled by another party

6. Members of the same family (brothers/sisters, whole or half blood; spouse; ancestors, lineal descendents)

Appendix E-1

J-LIST EXCEPTIONS

Articles of a class or kind listed below are excepted from the requirements of country of origin marking in accordance with the provisions of section 304(a)(3)(J), Tariff Act of 1930 as amended (19 U.S.C. 1304(a)(3)(J)). However, in the case of any article described in this list which is imported in a container, the outermost container in which the article ordinarily reaches the ultimate purchaser is required to be marked to indicate the origin of its contents in accordance with the requirements of subpart C of this part. All articles are listed in Treasury Decisions 49690, 49835 and 49896. A reference different from the foregoing indicates an amendment.

> Art, works of.
> Articles classified under subheadings
>   9810.00.15, 9810.00.25, 9810.00.40 and
>   9810.00.45, Harmonized Tariff Schedule of
>   the United States.
> Articles entered in good faith as antiques and
>   rejected as unauthentic.
> Bagging, waste.
> Bags, jute.
> Bands, steel.
> Beads, unstrung.
> Bearings, ball, 5/8-inch or less in diameter.
> Blanks, metal, to be plated.
> Bodies, harvest hat.
> Bolts, nuts, and washers.
> Briarwood in blocks.
> Briquettes, coal or coke.
> Buckles, 1 inch or less in greatest dimension.
> Burlap.
> Buttons.
> Cards, playing.
> Cellophane and celluloid in sheets, bands, or
>   strips.
> Chemicals, drugs, medicinal, and similar
>   substances, when imported in capsules,

pills, tablets, lozenges or troches.

Cigars and cigarettes.

Covers, straw bottle.

Dies, diamond wire, unmounted.

Dowels, wooden.

Effects, theatrical.

Eggs.

Feathers.

Firewood.

Flooring, not further manufactured than planed, tongued and grooved.

Flowers, artificial, except bunches.

Flowers, cut.

Glass, cut to shape and size for use in clocks, hand, pocket and purse mirrors, and other glass of similar shapes and sizes, not including lenses or watch crystals.

Glides, furniture, except glides with prongs.

Hairnets.

Hides, raw.

Hooks, fish (except snelled fish hooks).

Hoops (wood), barrel.

Laths.

Leather, except finished.

Livestock.

Lumber, sawed.

Metal bars, except concrete reinforcement bars; billets, blocks, blooms; ingots; pigs; plates; sheets, except galvinized sheets; shafting; slabs; and metal in similar forms.

Mica not further manufactured than cut or stamped to dimensions, shape or form.

Monuments.

Nails, spikes, and staples.

Natural products, such as vegetables, fruits, nuts berries and live or dead animals, fish and birds; all the foregoing which are in their natural state or not advanced in any manner further than is necessary for their safe transportation.

Nets, bottle wire.

Paper, newsprint.

Paper, stencil.

Paper, stock.

Parchment and vellum.

Parts for machines imported from same country as parts.

Pickets (wood).

Pins, tuning.

Plants, shrubs and other nursery stock.

Plugs, tie.

Poles, bamboo.

Posts (wood), fence.

Pulpwood.

Rags (including wiping rags.)

Rails, joint bars, and tie plates covered by subheadings 7302.10.10 through 7302.90.00, Harmonized Tariff Schedule of the United States.

Ribbon.

Rivets.

Rope, including wire rope; cordage; cords; twines, threads and yarns.

Scrap and waste.

Screws.

Shims, track.

Shingles (wood), bundles of (except bundles of red-cedar shingles).

Skins, fur, dressed or dyed.

Skins, raw fur.

Sponges.

Springs, watch.

Stamps, postage and revenue, and the articles covered in subheadings 9704.00.00 and 4807.00.00, Harmonized Tariff Schedule of the United States.

Staves, (wood) barrel.

Steel, hoop.

Sugar, maple.

Ties (wood), railroad.

Tides, not over 1 inch in greatest dimension.

Timbers, sawed.

Tips, penholder.

Trees, Christmas.

Weights, analytical and precision, in sets.

Wicking, candle.

Wire, except barbed.

Appendix E-2

GENERAL EXCEPTIONS

These exceptions DO NO APPLY to marking required by any other law. For example, marking required by other agencies, or special marking requirements for watches and clocks or other products.

J-List Exceptions - See list in CR 134.33
General Exceptions - CR 134.32

(a) Articles incapable of being marked
(b) Cannot be marked without injury
(c) Economically prohibitive to mark prior to shipment to U.S.
(d) Containers will indicate country of origin
(e) Crude substance
(f) Use by importer and not intended for sale
(g) To be processed in U.S., and marking would be concealed, etc. *Note exception to this exception in 134.36
(h) Ultimate purchaser knows c/o by circumstances of sale, or nature of articles
(i) Articles more than 20 years old
(j) Articles for IE or T&E
(k) Products of American fisheries which are duty-free
(l) Products of possessions of U.S.
(m) Products of U.S., exported and returned
(n) Articles exempt from duty - shipments valued < $200, gifts, etc.
(o) Economically prohibitive to mark after importation
(p) Art from a NAFTA country
(q) NAFTA goods in 6904.10, 8541 or 8542
(r) NAFTA U.S. goods returning after repair, etc.

Certain Repacked Articles - 134.25, .26 & .34
Articles changed by manufacture - 134.35

None of the exceptions apply to any article or container bearing markings which are misleading as to country of origin.

The containers for the above "excepted" articles must be marked, unless the container is also "excepted."

Appendix F-1

Foreign Assembler's Declaration

I, _____, declare that to the best of my knowledge and belief the _____ were assembled in whole or in part from fabricated components listed and described below, which are products of the United States:

Unit value at time				
Marks of identification/ Numbers	Description of component	Quantity and place of export from the U.S.	Port/date of export from U.S.	Name/address of manufacturer

Description of the operations preformed abroad on the exported components (in sufficient detail to enable Customs officers to determine whether the operations performed are within the purview of subheading 9802.00.80, Harmonized Tariff of the United States (19 USC 1202)(attach supplemental sheet if more space is required)):

Date:_____   Signature:_____

Address:_____   Capacity:_____

Appendix F-2

Importer's Endorsement
(for assembly operations under 9802.00.80)

I declare that to the best of my knowledge and belief the attached declaration, and any other information submitted herewith, or otherwise supplied or referred to, is correct in every respect and there has been compliance with all pertinent legal notes to the Harmonized Tariff Schedule of the United States (19 USC 1202).

Date:_____
Signature:_____

Address:_____
Capacity:_____

Index

A

Account Management System, 96
ACE see - Automated Control
Environment
ACS see - Automated Control
System
Actual Use, 33
ad valorum, 37
Additional U.S. Note of
Interpretation, 33
Administrative Review, 59
cause for denial, 67
clerical error, 61
import specialists, 59
other inadvertence, 62
reasons for rejection, 68
requests, 11, 62
ADP see - Automatic Data
Processing
AFR see- Application for Further
Review
Agreement on Trade in Civil
Aircraft, 53, 124, 125
Agriculture Dept. see - Dept. of
Agriculture
Andean Trade Preference Act
(ATPA), 122, 125
Anti-Dumping, 137
Application for Further Review
(AFR), 63
Assists, 20, 39, 44
ATF see - Bureau of Alchohol,
Tobacco and Firearms
ATPA see- Andean Trade
Preference
Act
Audits, 108
causes of, 108

Automated Commercial
Environment (ACE), 10
Automated Commercial System
(ACS), 1, 10
Automatic Data Processing
(ADP), 152

B

Bonded Warehouses, 54, 113, 141
classes, 141-142
quotas, 141
types, 10
Bonds, 11, 14
Bureau of Alcohol, Tobacco,
Firearms and Explosives
(BATFE), 86, 89
Bureau of Census, 14, 84

C

C&F see - Terms of Sale
Cargo Examinations, 11, 14-15
Caribbean Basin Initiative (CBI),
121-122, 125
Carnets, 54, 139
CBI see - Caribbean Basin
Initiative
CBP Form-19   60, 63
CBP Form-28   106
CBP Form-7501   65
Census Bureau see - Bureau of
Census
Certificate of Origin, 153, 154
Certificate of Registration, 132
CFR 19 see- Customs Regulations
CIF see - Terms of Sale

customs brokers, 13
examinations, 14-16
formal entry, 13-14
informal entry, 12
types, 10
Entry Summary, 13, 16, 37, 43,
65, 153,154
Environmental Protection Agency
(EPA), 88
EPA see - Environmental
Protection Agency
Essential Character, 29, 31
Exclusion Order, 134
Explanatory Notes to the HTSUS,
26

F

Fair Packaging and Labeling Act,
90
FAA see - Federal Aviation
Administration
FAC see - Foreign Assets Control
FAS see - Compact of Freely
Associated States
FDA see - Food & Drug
Administration
Federal Aviation Administration
(FAA), 54, 88, 124
Federal Register, 3, 34, 96
Federal Trade Commission (FTC),
90, 114
Field Import Specialists (FIS), 93
Fish & Wildlife Service (FWS), 87
FIS see - Field Import Specialists
FOB see - Terms of Sale
Food & Drug Administration
(FDA), 85-86, 89
Foreign Assests Control (FAC), 90
Foreign Trade Zone (FTZ), 10,
113, 140

Fraud, 103
19 USC 1592, 103
anti-dumping, 102
import specialists, 103
materiality, 101
negligence, 103
penalties, 104
special agent, 102
Freely Associated States see -
Compact of Freely Associated
States
FTC see - Federal Trade
Commission
FTZ see - Foreign Trade Zone
Fur Products Labeling Act, 90
FWS see - Fish & Wildlife
Service

G

General Accounting Office, 15
General Notes, 27, 150
General Rules of Interpretation
(GRI)
application, 28
GRI 1, 28
GRI 2(a), 29
GRI 2(b), 29
GRI 3(a), 29
GRI 3(b), 30
GRI 3(c), 30
GRI 4, 31
GRI 5(a), 31
GRI 5(b), 32
GRI 6, 32
Generalized System of Preference
(GSP), 67, 119, 125
GN see - General Notes
GRI see - General Rules of
Interpretation

H

Harmonized Tariff (HTSUS), 20, 25
 Additional U.S. Note of Interpretation, 33
 ADP, 152
 articles assembled abroad, 143- 145
 ATPA, 122
 CBI, 121-122
 Chapter 98, 50, 52
 Chapter 99, 52
 chemicals for dyes, 125
 civil aircraft, 124
 classification, 26
 construction, 27
 exemptions, 49
 Explanatory Notes, 26
 FAS, 123
 GN, 27, 126
 goods returned, 50-51
 government importations, 51
 GRI, 28-32
 GSP, 119-120
 misc. provisions, 53
 NAFTA, 126
 pharmaceutical products, 125
 rates of duty, 27
 samples, 51
 special program indicator, 125-126
 textile importation, 21
 TIB, 52
How to Design a Care Label, 90
HTSUS see - Harmonized Tariff

I

IFTA see - U.S./Israel Free Trade Agreement
Import Specialists, 15, 19, 23, 60, 101

Importer Self-Assessment, 96
Informed Compliance, 2-3
Internal Advice, 63, 98, 98
International Trade Administration (ITA), 138
International Trade Commission (ITC), 133
Investigations, 7
 CBP Form-28, 107
 commercial fraud teams, 106
 how generated, 106
 prior disclosure, 107
 request for information, 108
Invoices, 19
 considerations, 20
 Customs Regulations, 22
 import specialists, 23
 importer responsibility, 21
 informal entry, 12
 packing list, 23
 pro forma, 21
ITA see - Internal Trade Administration
ITC see - Internal Trade Commission

J

J-List, 75

L

Library of Congress, 130, 131
Liquidation, 60-61, 65
Liquidation Notice see Courtesy Notice of Liquidation

M

Marking
 containers, 76
 country of origin, 16, 72
 customs brokers, 11

GOVERNMENT PUBLICATIONS

Harmonized Tariff Schedule of the United States (HTSUS)

Government-issued import tariff for use in classifying imported merchandise.

Required text for importer's compliance using 'reasonable care' guidelines.

Subscription service for the calendar year of publication. All government-published updates will be sent FREE.

LOOSELEAF edition includes shrinkwrapped pages and all updates.
DELUXE edition includes looseleaf pages (with all updates), heavy-duty binders and indexing tabs.

Source material for the Customs Broker Exam

PN 0511-0101
  2005 HTSUS - Looseleaf......................$ 94.00
PN 0511-0102
  2005 HTSUS - Deluxe $136.00
PN 0540-0101
  2005 HTSUS on CD-Rom.....................$ 89.00

Schedule B -
Statistical Classification for Exports

Statistical classification of commodities exported from the United States. For use by shippers in reporting export shipments from the U.S.

Required text for exporter's compliance.

Subscription service for the calendar year of publication. All government-published updates will be sent FREE.

2005 Updates Only
For those with 2001 editions or earlier, order full book (deluxe, looseleaf, or CD-ROM.) If you previously ordered the 2002 edition with updates through 2004, **save money** and order "updates only" for 2005.

LOOSELEAF edition includes shrinkwrapped pages and all updates.
DELUXE edition includes looseleaf pages (with all updates), heavy-duty binder and indexing tabs.

PN 0215-0201
  2002 Schedule B - Looseleaf............$135.00
PN 0215-0202
  2002 Schedule B - Deluxe $157.00
PN 0515-0203
  2005 Schedule B Updates Only ....$ 59.00
PN 0540-0201
  2005 Schedule B on CD-Rom...........$ 89.00

U.S. Customs Regulations

19 Code of Federal Regulations, Chapter 1, Parts 1-199

Government-issued reference contains all U.S. Customs Regulations for importers, brokers, and transportation-related companies.

Required text for importer's compliance using 'reasonable care' guidelines.

Subscription service for the calendar year of publication. All government-published updates will be sent FREE.

LOOSELEAF edition includes shrinkwrapped pages and all updates.
DELUXE edition includes looseleaf pages (with all updates), heavy-duty binders and indexing tabs.

Source material for the Customs Broker Exam.

PN 0411-0201
  2004 Customs Regs - Looseleaf.......$175.00
PN 0411-0202
  2004 Customs Regs - Deluxe $195.00
PN 0511-0203
  2005 Updates Only...........................$ 69.00
PN 0540-0301
  2005 Customs Regs on CD-Rom.....$ 89.00

Export Administration Regulations

A compilation of official regulations and policies governing the export licensing of commodities and technical data.

Required text for exporter's compliance.

Subscription service for the calendar year of publication. All government-published updates will be sent FREE.

LOOSELEAF edition includes shrinkwrapped pages and all updates.
DELUXE edition includes looseleaf pages (with all updates), heavy-duty binders and indexing tabs.

PN 0515-0101
  2005 Export Regs. - Looseleaf $165.00
PN 0515-0102
  2005 Export Regs. - Deluxe..............$209.00
PN 0540-0401
  2005 Export Regs. on CD-Rom ....$ 89.00

Plus...
- Importer's Compliance Package
- Federal Maritime Regulations
- Explanatory Notes to the HTSUS
- Code of Federal Regulations Titles
- Exporter's Compliance Package
- Policy and Procedure Manual
- The Essential Import Dictionary
- *And much, much more!*
- On-Line Learning Programs
- C-TPAT Procedure Manual
- Customs Broker Study Program

System Requirements: *VGA Monitor, 64 meg RAM, WIN 98/00/ME/NT/XP*
Government publications require pre-payment. • All prices subject to change.
Products shipped in one business day immediately upon release.

Boskage Commerce Publications, Ltd.   •   888-880-4088   •   www.boskage.com

OneSource Digital Library

A Customs & International Trade Reference Library

- Advanced search capabilities. • Hyperlinked references for quick cross-checking.
- Immediate free updates throughout the calendar year.

Choose one - or purchase a combined package and save!

Import Package

10 modules for only $249⁰⁰
PN 0540-6601

The Harmonized Tariff of the U.S. - 2005 HTSUS for use in determining classification and rate of duty, quota, restrictions, and special programs.

U.S. Customs Regulations - 19 CFR Chapter I, Parts 1-199. All pertinent government import regulations.

Importer Compliance - Self-Assessment Handbook, "Reasonable Care" Checklist, and Recordkeeping Compliance Handbook.

Importing Basics - Includes "Howdy, Duty!" and U.S. Customs "Importing into the U.S."

FTZ/Bonded Warehouse - Learn the ins and outs of U.S. Customs bonded warehouses and foreign trade zones and save money.

U.S. Commercial Directives - Contains rulings, instructions on policy and procedure, and regulation interpretations.

Duty Drawback - U.S. Customs advice on filing for drawback, records required, and regulations that cover this profitable procedure.

NAFTA - Includes text of "When You HAFTA do NAFTA" and "NAFTA: A Guide to Customs Procedure".

Valuation and Classification - "Basic Principles of Tariff Classification" and "U.S. Customs Valuation Encyclopedia."

Trade and Tariff Acts - Act of 1930, 1994 General Agreement on Tariffs and Trade, and the Trade Agreement Act of 1979.

Export Package

7 modules for only $249⁰⁰
PN 0540-6701

Schedule B - Current statistical classification for goods leaving the U.S.

Export Regulations - The official Export Administration Regulations governing exportation.

Guide to Exporting - Develop export strategy, service exports, learn ways to finance transactions, and create solid agreements.

Freight Fwd/Ocean Exporter - FMC regulations, Chpt 46, Parts 500-end.

Duty Drawback - U.S. Customs advice on filing for drawback, records required, and regulations that cover this profitable procedure.

FTZ/Bonded Warehouse - Learn the ins and outs of U.S. Customs bonded warehouses and foreign trade zones and save money.

ITAR - International Traffic in Arms Regulations - 22 CFR, Parts 120-130. Issued by the Office of Defense Trade Controls, describes all items requiring special licensing for exportation.

P.I.E.
Pocket Import Expert
Only $89⁰⁰ PN 0540-1701
Import advice on all HTSUS Chapters. Includes complete 2005 HTSUS tariff.

Customs Rulings
Only $300⁰⁰ PN 0540-1501
Add this module to any package or buy alone!

Select the option right for you!

Any one module ....*Buy one module, or add one module to any package*..**$ 89.00**

Import Package ....*Includes 10 import publications at one low price* **$249.00**

Export Package......................*Includes 7 export publications at one low price* **$249.00**

Import/Export Combo ....*Includes both import and export packages*.................... **$429.00**

Network License ....*Unlimited users on one network for any package* **$100.00**

System Requirements: VGA Monitor, 64 meg RAM, WIN 98/00/ME/NT/XP
Government publications require pre-payment. • **All prices subject to change.**
Products shipped in one business day immediately upon release.

Boskage Commerce Publications, Ltd.   •   888-880-4088   •   www.boskage.com